Darren Callahan's
SALAMANDER LAKE

Battery Filmtext

The Collected Screenplays of Darren Callahan
Limited Edition Series

Published in the United States of America by Battery Filmtext

Printed in the United States of America

Battery Filmtext and its logo are registered trademarks of
HCC Limited Release

Design, Materials, and Essay Content © Battery Filmtext, Norman Berklein
Battery Filmtext, Los Angeles, California, U.S.A.
www.batteryfilmtext.com

Screenplay © Darren Callahan, All Rights Reserved

The Library of Congress Catalog
Callahan, Darren
Collected Screenplays: Vol. 17: SALAMANDER LAKE
1st ed. in the United States of America
p. cm.

ISBN 9798666092767

BATTERY FILMTEXT
publishes screenplays
(both produced and unproduced)
that are compelling examples of
thoughtful genre writing. Our focus is on
horror, exploitation, and vintage suspense/thriller.

Our editions are typically part of a limited edition series focused on
a single screenwriter. We bring attention to the stories we admire,
regardless of whether that story or its author are well-known.

In keeping the text as close to the authoring experience as possible,
we publish our scripts in draft form, sometimes with flaws or
typos intact, and without scene numbers.
Should a published screenplay evolve with later drafts,
editions are republished.

SALAMANDER LAKE
is a (slightly more expensive) Roger Corman movie,
much like Humanoids from the Deep (1980), or Universal's
Creature from the Black Lagoon (1954), except with old people.
You read that right. Old people. Callahan takes a somewhat controversial
stance with a story that nearly exclusively features the elderly and then
has absolutely no problem killing them off in large swaths. Set in the
heartland of America, there are also political jabs, satire, and digs on
everything from immigration reform to racist conspiracy theories.
Similar to his works The Battle for Carlyle or All These Demons,
Callahan easily threads a dozen major characters into perfectly paced
back-and-forth action set pieces that ultimately time out into one fiery
climax. Citing the formula of 1970s Irwin Allen disaster pics,
this little number is sure to not win any awards,
but it certainly is a crowd-pleaser.

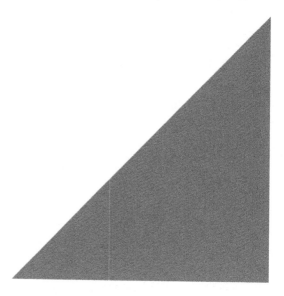

INT. COMMUNITY CENTER - NIGHT

A rustic Community Center, decked for the holidays with lights and a banner.

"MERRY CHRISTMAS, GRASSY GLADE!"

A JAZZ COMBO plays for--

--the RESIDENTS. And you're about to meet a lot of them. Like in "Magnolia" or "The Towering Inferno" or "The Great Escape" or "Love Actually." So be patient. It'll work.

Almost everyone is above the age of 60, some into their 80s or 90s. Singles, couples, women in dresses, men in suits.

Laughter, drinks, dancing.

Under a hanging mistletoe:

ARPY ADAMS -- 70s, dyed hair, abundant jewelry.

She kisses her husband:

JESSE ADAMS -- 70s, hang-dog face, wavy hair.

Claps and cheers.

FAVOR ON:

EVELYN ADAMS -- 40s, a younger version of her mother. Pale, a little sad, who gazes on her parents with absolute adoration.

At a table, CARD PLAYERS throw down a hand, groan in frustration. It's the end of a cut-throat game featuring:

DON LE MANS -- 70s, gray beard, bow-tie -- who rakes in his winnings.

                    DON
          Ha, ha, hey! Next time, fellows,
          next time.

Away from the music and celebration:

HERB WARREN -- 60s, rugged, round face -- who mushes-up food for his wife:

LINDA WARREN -- 70s, in a wheelchair, faraway look, lost.

MOVE TO:

The center's foyer.

JIMMIE CALVIN -- 30s, jacket and cowboy hat.

FRED KENT -- 30s, ex-Marine in too-tight dress blues.

> JIMMIE
> Where's Sidney?

Fred hitches a thumb across the main room towards:

SIDNEY REED -- early 70s, mercurial, ladies man, as he delivers a plate of food to:

PEGGY MARSH -- late 60s, beautiful face, unfortunate wig, seated near the stage.

> JIMMIE (CONT'D)
> Sidney knows, right? He knows it's tonight?

> FRED
> He knows. Calm down, Jimmie. He's just takin' his time.

Fred fixes Jimmie's collar.

> JIMMIE
> Well he'd better do it soon.

EXT. COMMUNITY CENTER - NIGHT

A black limousine rolls into the parking lot.

Stops at the snow-covered steps of the Community Center.

INT. LIMOUSINE - NIGHT

Inside the limo:

ROY ALMA -- 50s, butch, expensive blue suit and power tie.

VIRGIL HAMLIN -- 40s, cheap tie and baggy blazer, eyes on his wristwatch.

VICTORIA and SHIRLEY EVANS -- twin sisters in their late 20s.

Roy flattens his hair, fiddles with his tie.

> ROY
> I look all right?

                    VICTORIA | SHIRLEY
        Yes, Roy.

                    ROY
        This tie's too damn tight.

ictoria undoes the knot for him, re-ties.

                    VIRGIL
        It's just five minutes, Roy. You
        shouldn't shake hands. Five and
        then go.

                    ROY
        How far to Turnersville?

                    VIRGIL
        50 minutes.

                    ROY
        Jesus. It's almost nine.
        Turnersville goin' that late?

                    VIRGIL
        Yes, I checked it. But we can't
        stay too long. Keep it light. In
        and out.

e caresses Victoria on the thigh as she finishes his tie,
nen gives Shirley a squeeze.

                    ROY
        In and out.

JT. COMMUNITY CENTER - NIGHT

niformed STAFF collects supper dishes.

ne BLONDE WAITER -- 20s, baby face -- SNATCHES the meal
rom Herb Warren's hands and replaces it with a bowl of ice
ream.

                    HERB
        Thank you.

it he wasn't actually done.

erb holds out the spoon for Linda.

                    HERB (CONT'D)
          Here you go, y lovely. A tasty
          treat for your tummy.

Linda barely opens her mouth.

EXT. COMMUNITY CENTER - NIGHT

Roy helps the Evans sisters up the Community Center steps.
Each takes one of his arms and, in the wrong footwear, the
women tread lightly.

                         ROY
          That's it, darlins. Watch the ice.
          It's slippery. There ya go.

Virgil shuffles out of the limo, slams the door.

Victoria SLIPS! Roy CATCHES her.

Both laugh.

                    ROY (CONT'D)
          I tol' you. I tol' you!

                      VICTORIA
          I almost slipped!

                         ROY
          You did, you did, I saw it.

He kisses her cheek.

                    ROY (CONT'D)
          And one for you.

A second kiss on the other sister's forehead.

INT. COMMUNITY CENTER - NIGHT

The front doors of the Community Center WHOOSH open.

Jimmie and Fred spring to attention.

                       JIMMIE
          Mr. Alma! Glad you made it in this
          weather.

                         ROY
          Call me Roy. Who's this?

                    JIMMIE
This is Fred. Kent.

                    ROY
          (re: the uniform)
I like the fashion, Mr. Kent. How
long did you serve?

                    FRED
Six years active. Two deployments.

                    ROY
I was an Navy man. Nice to see a
fellow patriot.
          (re: the party)
How many inside?

irgil struggles to close the doors, stuck in snow.

                    JIMMIE
Oh, about 75.

                    ROY
And Mr. Reed?

                    FRED
I think he's gonna do it during
dessert.

                    ROY
What's our countdown?

                    JIMMIE
Any moment.

                    FRED
Any moment.

                    ROY
All right. Go get him. I want to
talk.

ed hops away to retrieve Sidney Reed.

                    ROY (CONT'D)
Jimmie Calvin, this is Victoria.
This is Shirley. The Evans
sisters. You may have seen them at
the county fair.

                    JIMMIE
The singers, yes, very talented.

The sisters blush.

>   ROY
>   And this is Virgil Hamlin.

Virgil finally gets the doors shut, checks the time.

>   ROY (CONT'D)
>   He'll be local, once we get
>   rollin'.

In the party fray, Don Le Mans wins another hand of cards.

>   DON
>   Ha, ha, hey! Whatduya know about
>   that!

He scoops in the money.

Another CARD PLAYER takes issue.

>   CARD PLAYER
>   You got a system, Le Mans! Old
>   fart's got a system.

>   DON
>   Just my brains, gentleman.

>   CARD PLAYER
>   You don't have any brains.

>   DON
>   Working better than your ol' noggin
>   tonight. Ha, ha, hey!

Across the way, Fred taps Sidney Reed's shoulder.

>   FRED
>   It's, uh...

>   SIDNEY
>   He's here?

Fred points. Sidney turns to Peggy.

>   SIDNEY (CONT'D)
>   Will you be all right without me
>   for a moment, Peggy?

>   PEGGY
>   Only if you bring me another drink!

idney takes her hand, kisses it.

> SIDNEY
> It's a deal.

ises, smiles, departs with Fred.

> SIDNEY (CONT'D)
> (aside)
> Newly widowed. And those tits!

ack in the foyer, Sidney greets Roy.

> ROY
> Good to see you, Sid.

andshakes.

> SIDNEY
> Uh, I haven't started yet.

oy puts a fatherly hand on Sidney's shoulder.

> ROY
> Sid, you got a way with these
> people. You know I can't go in
> there until you've done your warm
> up. I've got to be in Turnersville
> in an hour.
> (softer)
> So get your mind off the pussy and
> let's make some money. Okay?

dney nods. Eager to please.

eturns into the heart of the Community Center.

dney weaves through the party until he reached the stage.

eps onto the riser, shushes the Jazz Combo.

ps the microphone.

> SIDNEY
> Hello. Hello? Can y'all hear me?

e Residents respond.

> RESIDENTS
> Yes!

                    SIDNEY
          Oh, you can? Okay, good. Everyone
          got their hearing aids in?

Laughs.

                    SIDNEY (CONT'D)
          Ladies and Gentlemen of the Grassy
          Glade Private Community... You are
          my neighbors, my friends, and, in
          these closing chapters of our
          spectacular lives... I want you to
          remember. This place is sacred.
          Grassy Glade is sacred. We have 18
          holes of golf right out that door.
          We have rivers and streams. We
          have good old Salamander Lake for
          our fishing, our boating, and our
          relaxation on hot summer days. In
          the fall, we have all the beautiful
          foliage that Appalachia has to
          offer...

In the corridor, Roy rolls his eyes.

                    ROY
          Jesus... Who does he think he is,
          Henry David Fucking Thoreau?

                    SIDNEY
          ...hills... mountains... beautiful
          in the peaceful blowing of a
          winter's snow on a Christmas Eve.
          I love it here. I love it. Clap
          if you love it here.

The Residents CLAP enthusiastically.

                    SIDNEY (CONT'D)
          Safe, too. No outsiders except for
          our friends and families and our
          wonderful staff. Here we keep our
          independence and HERE... is where
          we have chosen to finish out our
          years. The Grassy Glade Private
          Community. As beautiful a place
          that has ever been.

Virgil checks the time.

Impatient, Roy marches to brink of the main room, takes a
position where Sidney can see him.

idney notes it.

                    SIDNEY (CONT'D)
          Uh, as the Chairman of the Board, I
          am always on the lookout for
          opportunity.

arpy spots Roy Alma. Taps her husband Jesse on the
noulder.

esse and Evelyn both glance over.

                    HARPY
               (soft)
          Is that who I think it is?

esse nods.

velyn also catches sight of Jimmie Calvin, who waves at
er.

                    SIDNEY
          So I want to take this happy moment
          when we're all together to announce
          a new partnership. Tanner Chemical
          of Chattanooga, Tennessee has
          honored us with an idea--

                    DON
               (under breath)
          --Oh, no--

                    SIDNEY
          --to test an anti-algae formula
          within our waterways, which will
          clean Salamander Lake once and for
          all of the mucky-muck that we hate.
          Now, I'm no scientist, so, to
          answer your questions, Roy Alma,
          the President of Tanner Chemical,
          has driven all this way--

estures.

l eyes on Roy.

                    SIDNEY (CONT'D)
          --to tell us a little bit more
          about this exciting improvement.
          Let's give him a big Grassy Glade,
          Merry Christmas welcome!

Into this fanfare, Roy advances, his best smile and parade-waves. A round of handshakes as he takes the stage.

>   ROY
>   Good evening, people of Grassy
>   Glade! It was not my intention to
>   disrupt your Christmas party, but I
>   am happy to have some of that
>   delicious ice cream and answer your
>   questions. There will be a public
>   meeting in March with details, but
>   I wanted to thank you directly for
>   your participation. This idea was
>   approved unanimously by your Board
>   of Directors. Special thanks to
>   Sid for shepherding it through. As
>   you may have read in the papers,
>   Tanner Chemical is known for
>   success. We've had 12 trials
>   around the Great Smoky Mountains
>   for various innovations and we have
>   completely changed lives for the
>   better, for the better!

Evelyn Adams dips towards her mother, Harpy.

>   EVELYN
>   (soft)
>   That's not what I read.

>   ROY
>   Blue green algae, also known as
>   cyanobacteria, are microscopic, but
>   not your friend. Some call them
>   planktonic algae. These come with
>   microcystin and toxins. These
>   contaminate lakes and pond water
>   and are a hazard to all life --
>   particularly human life. Our
>   top-notch team -- from John
>   Hopkins, Carnegie Mellon, and
>   Vanderbilt -- use the best science
>   to achieve the best result. That's
>   what Tanner is about! And, we are
>   prepared to offer each of you
>   specific, per-household
>   compensation.

Big smiles.

                    ROY (CONT'D)
          What we want you to have the best
          water on the planet. For the best
          people in these United States. And
          you have my promise. Nothing is
          going to be done to harm a single
          silver hair on your Proud American
          heads.

                                        FADE TO BLACK.

TITLE CARD: "SIX MONTHS LATER"

                                        FADE IN ON:

EXT. LAKE - DAY

RALPH DOREM -- 60s, in vest and pants, ball-cap, rod slung
over the side of a Pond Prowler fishing boat.

He waits patiently for a bite.

Listens to birds, the rustling trees on the nearby
shoreline.

A tug!

                    RALPH
          Ohp. Yep. There we go. There we
          go.

He flicks his rod, reels it in.

                    RALPH (CONT'D)
          Come to papa. That's it.

He lifts a smallmouth bass out of the lake.

                    RALPH (CONT'D)
          Well, aren't ye pretty? Yep. Oh
          ya.

Hauls it onto the boat.

It's big. Really big. Plump, perfect.

INT. GENERAL STORE - DAY

Jesse Adams wanders the aisles of Grassy Glade's General
Store.

Behind the counter:

LEO BARRY -- 30s, dark beard, handsome, a bit heavy, in flannel shirt, kind face.

Jesse finds a display of fishing lures.

                    LEO
          Help you find somethin', Jesse?

                    JESSE
          Nope. I got it.

                    LEO
          Hey, we can get those lures
          personalized now. If you want to
          inscribe something on the plate.

                    JESSE
          Why? It's just goin' in the water.

                    LEO
          I don't know. Something fun. "I'm
          hooked on you, baby."

                    JESSE
          I'll think about it.

He picks out a couple plain-jane lures.

                    JESSE (CONT'D)
          These'll do. I don't need anything
          fancy with they way they been
          biting.

                    LEO
          Yeah, there's quite the stock this
          year. Better than I can ever
          remember.

                    JESSE
          Must be all that Tanner Chemistry.

Leo nods, rings up the lures.

                    LEO
          Your daughter here for the 4th?

                    JESSE
          She will be.

                    LEO
          She still single?

                    JESSE
          Evelyn's single, then she's not,
          then she's single again. Then
          she's not.

    eo bags Jesse's lures, smiles.

                    LEO
          Then I better get going.

                    JESSE
          I guess you'd better.

    esse leaves with a grin.

    XT. LAKE - SHORELINE - DAY

    irgil Hamlin, on the rocky shore of Salamander Lake.

    lipboard. Hard-hat. Eyes to his watch.

)V:
    EVEN WORKERS -- employees of Tanner Chemical -- atop a 20'
    20' platform a short distance away, in the water.

)sitioned in the center--

    -A DRILL, surrounded by metal cage.

    irgil's cell rings.

                    VIRGIL
          Hamlin.

                    ROY
               (over phone)
          Have they started yet?

                    VIRGIL
          We're just about to place the
          drill, Mr. Alma.

                    ROY
          Go six feet deeper than we planned.

                    VIRGIL
          We're already goin' down 25.

                         ROY
          Push it.

Virgil, unsure.

                         VIRGIL
          I don't want to damage the drill.

                         ROY
          Turnersville shows we might need to
          go deeper. Good luck.

Click.

Virgil pockets his phone, pulls a walkie-talkie.

                         VIRGIL
          Hamlin here.

EXT. LAKE - PLATFORM - DAY - SAME MOMENT

RUDY GALVAN -- 30s, in coveralls, wet to his knees --
answers Virgil's transmission.

                         RUDY
          Go for Rudy.

                         VIRGIL
                    (over speaker)
          Alma wants it six feet deeper.
                    (beat)
          You gonna argue it?

                         RUDY
          No, sir.

Rudy tosses his walkie-talkie into a bin. Turns to the
other six Workers.

                         RUDY (CONT'D)
          Ready?

Nods.

                         RUDY (CONT'D)
          Fire it up.

ROOOOOM!

The drill charges to life--

XT. LAKE - SHORELINE - DAY - SAME MOMENT

-Satisfied, Virgil walks from the shore to his pick-up.

ide decal reads:

TANNER CHEMICAL"

aiting for him -- Jimmie Calvin and Fred Kent.

                    FRED
          Is there a problem?

                    VIRGIL
          No.

e notes the time.

                    JIMMIE
                (re: drill)
          That thing's pretty loud.

                    VIRGIL
          It has to go down 13 feet through
          the water and then 31 more feet
          through the bed.

                    FRED
          How will they see what they're
          doing?

                    VIRGIL
          There's a camera. It will be
          turned on when it reaches the
          aphotic zone.
                (clarifying)
          The depth where the light stops.

XT. LAKE - UNDERWATER - DAY

he drill cuts.

irs the darkening water, disperses the fish.

light SWITCHES ON when the sunlight snuffs.

T. LAKE - PLATFORM - DAY

dy checks a monitor on the platform.

Dials-in the camera image.

Watches the drill CONNECT with the lake bottom.

EXT. LAKE - SHORELINE - DAY

Fred watches the work on the platform.

Virgil leans on the truck.

Jimmie joins him.

> VIRGIL
> Salamander is a crater lake.
> Created by an extraterrestrial
> impact.

> FRED
> A spaceship?

> VIRGIL
> A meteor. Hit 10,000 years ago,
> and now, you have a lake.

> JIMMIE
> You sure do know a lot about lakes.

> FRED
> Say, why you drillin', if you're
> just fixin' the algae?

> VIRGIL
> ...Oh, well... we just want to make
> sure there are no adverse
> environmental effects. The best
> way is a deep sample from the bed.

Nods from Fred and Jimmie.

Though they really don't understand.

EXT. LAKE - PLATFORM - DAY

Rudy watches the drill spin into the silt of the lake.

Silent. Stirs up sand and stone.

Checks a descending gauge:

"26 FT."

27 FT."

28 FT."

uddenly-!

-the drill CATCHES.

he platform SHUDDERS.

orkers GRAB the rails.

he gauge -- stuck at "29 FT."

                    RUDY
          Shit. Pull it up.

 Worker throws a lever.

he drill reverses.

ıdy scans the shore, to Virgil, Fred, and Jimmie.

e gestures -- a hand cuts over his throat -- a "no go."

KT. LAKE - SHORELINE - DAY - SAME MOMENT

ırgil catches Rudy's signal.

                    VIRGIL
          Damn.

                    FRED
          Somethin' go wrong?

ırgil clicks on his walkie-talkie.

                    VIRGIL
               (into radio)
          What's happening?

                    RUDY
               (over radio)
          Musta hit rock. Broke the drill.
          Looks like it's gonna be a long
          night.

INT. WARREN HOUSE - KITCHEN - NIGHT

Herb Warren crosses through his comfortable home until he reaches the kitchen.

Linda Warren sits at the dining table, belted in a chair. Weak, inattentive, a plate of apple sauce in front of her.

Herb sits. Breathes.

                    HERB
          Are you ready for bed?

No reaction.

                    HERB (CONT'D)
          Nurse Tina's comin' tomorrow.   I
          need to run some errands.

No reaction.

Herb looks at his lap. Sighs.

                    HERB (CONT'D)
          Okay... let's get you to bed, my
          lovely.

INT. CASTLE RESTAURANT - NIGHT

Don Le Mans enters the Castle Restaurant -- small town fanc dining -- round tables, kitchen, bar.

Crowded with SENIOR CITIZENS.

Don navigates to the corner, where Fred Kent and Jimmie Calvin drink beer in a booth.

Without asking, Don slides in.

                    DON
          Gentlemen. You look exhausted.   Do
          you, perhaps--

Takes out a deck of playing cards.

                    DON (CONT'D)
          --care for a game?

                    JIMMIE
          Forget it, Le Mans. We know all
          about you.

DON
What! The three of us have never had a tourney. And it's well. Past. Time.

FRED
It's only nine o'clock.

DON
I mean time the time for you to win some money from Don Le Mans.

JIMMIE
No one ever wins off you. Look, I only have 15 bucks and you ain't takin' it.

DON
Quarter stakes.

JIMMIE
I said you ain't takin' it.

DON
What's the problem? Tanner not paying you enough to be their lackeys?

FRED
We get paid plenty.

JIMMIE
And we're not lackeys.

on cuts the deck.

DON
Ha, ha, hey! All right, dime a game.

JIMMIE
I ain't got change.

DON
Five card stud?

FRED
Go back to Vegas, Le Mans.

JIMMIE
Yeah, pick on someone your own age.

EXT. LAKE - UNDERWATER - NIGHT

The drill, stuck in the floor of Lake Salamander like the
Sword in the Stone.

EXT. LAKE - PLATFORM - NIGHT - SAME MOMENT

Under lamp-light, Rudy and the Workers lower a cable into
the water.

A FIT WORKER in a wet suit prepares.

                    RUDY
          You set?

A nod from the Fit Worker.

                    RUDY (CONT'D)
          Lock the rigging on the hitch, give
          the rope three tugs. We'll weld
          that some-bitch back together
          onshore.

EXT. LAKE - UNDERWATER - NIGHT - CONTINUOUS

The Fit Worker DIVES into the dark lake.

Paddles down towards the broken drill.

Lights an underwater lamp, trains it on the ground.

Drags the rigging behind him.

INT. MARSH HOUSE - NIGHT

In the house of Peggy Marsh, the beautiful older woman
travels her long hallway to a comfortable Guest Room.

She holds at the door until she spots:

Virgil Hamlin, shirt off. Sets his watch on a dresser.

At first, Virgil doesn't notice her gaze.

                    VIRGIL
          Oh! I'm sorry. I shoulda shut the
          door. I'm not used to this Bed &
          Breakfast stuff.

                         PEGGY
          No apology necessary, Mr. Hamlin.
          Have you got everything you need?

                         VIRGIL
          All set.

                         PEGGY
          Your bathroom is right through that
          door. Mine's the other side of the
          house. If you need anything --
          anything at all -- just knock.
          Don't be shy now, ya hear?

                         VIRGIL
          'Night.

eggy gives a lingering look at the man's chest, then
eturns down the hallway.

NT. MARSH HOUSE - MASTER BATH - NIGHT

eggy enters her master bathroom.

: the mirror, she slips off her clothes, reveals her
urves.

eaching up, she draws the pins out of her hair.

emoves her wig.

e is nearly bald.

T. LAKE - UNDERWATER - NIGHT

ep underwater, the Fit Worker has reached the broken
ill.

tempts to hitch the rigging.

 drops his lamp!

unces on the lake bottom.

ght sprays the CRACK caused by the drill.

e Fit Worker ties off the rope.

nds to retrieve the lamp--

--RUMBLE!

The lake floor cracks wide!

Right at the drill spot.

The drill SLIPS down!

The Fit Worker reaches out -- GRABS the broken drill by its jagged top, to halt its fall.

The jagged metal SLICES his hand!

Blood EXPLODES in slow motion and he winces.

The drill FALLS through the fissure.

Disappears into darkness.

The Fit Worker hugs his injured hand.

The rope -- still tied to the drill -- sways, taut.

He maneuvers the rope. Attempts to rescue the drill from the fissure.

All his strength.

Winds the rope around his other hand. PULLS.

No good.

He kicks backwards. Assesses.

Resigned, he swims towards the surface.

EXT. LAKE - PLATFORM - NIGHT - CONTINUOUS

Rudy watches the rigging draped over the platform.

                    RUDY
          Did you feel something? That
          wasn't a tug.

EXT. LAKE - UNDERWATER - NIGHT - CONTINUOUS

The Fit Worker continues to climb.

Follows the rope up.

ehind him!

he fissure ERUPTS.

idens another six feet.

he sharp drill BREAKS from its catch and--

-LAUNCHES from the basin against the tension of the igging.

he drill SPEARS the Fit Worker right through his chest!

nstantly dead, his body levels.

lood colors the water.

XT. LAKE - PLATFORM - NIGHT - CONTINUOUS

he platform SHAKES with the release of the drill.

udy turns to the Workers.

                    RUDY
          Feel that?

XT. LAKE - UNDERWATER - NIGHT - CONTINUOUS

he fissure is now wide.

rom under the bottom of the lake...

.emerges...

.a HUMANOID CREATURE.

aly, larger than an average man. Thick legs, strong arms, narp teeth, black eyes. Enormous head.

he Creature swims free of the fissure.

ehind...

.a second Creature.

en a THIRD.

en a FOURTH.

EXT. LAKE - PLATFORM - NIGHT - CONTINUOUS

The Workers haul the rigging. Rudy directs.

                    RUDY
          Pull! Pull!

Rudy stretches to snare the rigging.

                    RUDY (CONT'D)
          Come on. Pull!

The Workers struggle against the weight.

At last, the tip of the drill pierces the surface.

                    RUDY (CONT'D)
          That's it! Keep pulling.

At the first sight of the Fit Worker's body, a shish kabob-

--a SHORT WORKER let's go of the rope. Shock hits.

                    RUDY (CONT'D)
          Oh, Jesus. Get him up. Get him
          up!

The Workers snap into action.

Rudy drops his pole, moves to help.

Workers lift the impaled Fit Worker onto the platform.

So occupied with the task...

...they do not see...

...Creatures break the surface on the opposite side of the
platform. The lake bubbles with a half-dozen more.

EXT. LAKE - SHORELINE - NIGHT - CONTINUOUS

From the nearby shore, the platform rocks with--

--an attack!

The Creatures DECIMATE Rudy and his Workers.

It's a bloodbath.

                                        DISSOLVE TO:

XT. LAKE - SHORELINE - DAWN

irgil Hamlin arrives at the shoreline, same spot as before.

arks his truck. Steps out.

ne platform bobbles in the morning light.

akes him a moment to realize.

omething is not right.

irgil YANKS a tool box from the truck's bed. Draws out
inoculars.

DV:
ne platform -- covered in blood and bodies.

> VIRGIL
> Oh my God.

JT. LAKE HOUSE - DAWN

NOCKS on the door of a high-dollar lake house.

idney Reed rouses from sleep.

n pajamas, he answers his front door to find--

-Virgil Hamlin, in a panic.

> VIRGIL
> We have to make a call.

JT. LAKE HOUSE - KITCHEN - DAWN

n Sidney's lake house kitchen, Sidney and Virgil hover over
speakerphone.

> ROY
> (over speaker)
> You know these people, Sid. What's
> your take?

> SIDNEY
> They'll ask questions. We're old,
> but we're not dumb. They'll ask
> how an algae study killed seven
> people.

Virgil checks his watch.

> VIRGIL
> I... think we should report this to
> the local sheriff--

> ROY
> --No, Virgil. No. Sheriff's make
> news. What about Fred Kent?
> Marines follow orders. Throw a
> bunch of money at him. I want you
> both to get down to the lake and
> clean it up. By ten o'clock.
> Before someone finds the goddamn
> thing.

EXT. LAKE - SHORELINE - DAWN

Fisherman Ralph Dorem -- bright vest and heavy pants --
whistles as he carries his rod high through the lake brush.

Sets down his bait box by the shoreline, opens it.

Eyes up to the morning sun over the faraway hills.

When he bends to dig into his bait box...

...he raises up and, for the first time, notices--

--the platform on the water.

Squints.

Sets down his rod.

Moves to the lapping water.

Squints tighter.

The platform, silhouetted, sun on the other side, but...

He makes out the shapes of twisted arms and bent legs.

In his boots and fishing pants, Ralph wades out to his
knees.

> RALPH
> Hello? Hey! Y'all all right?

Water rocks the platform. No reply.

alph moves out to his waist.

                    RALPH (CONT'D)
          Speak!

othing.

oncerned, Ralph returns to dry land.

y his bait box--

-a Creature!

rouched over the box.

or a second, Ralph considers -- is this a man?

                    RALPH (CONT'D)
          Who are you?

he Creature turns its big head.

n its ugly snout -- a handful of bait, mid-bite.

ow Ralph knows for certain. This is not a man.

                    RALPH (CONT'D)
          Oh, Jesus.

e reverses into the water.

acks-in up to his knees.

atches the Creature devour his bait.

alph doesn't know what to do.

inks. Clenches his jaw.

it no time to act.

 second Creature! Buried in the lake.

aps its leathery arms around Ralph's body and--

JERKS him down into the shallows!

T. COUNTRY ROAD - DAY

Toyota Corolla winds a country road.

A sign:

"GRASSY GRADE PRIVATE RETIREMENT COMMUNITY"

Smaller print:

"All Visitors Must Register"

EXT. VISITOR'S CENTER - DAY

The Corolla parks at a small white hut.

Alongside, a wrought-iron gate blocks a two-lane road.

Sign:

"VISITOR'S CENTER"

Engine off, out steps Evelyn Adams, in jeans and tee-shirt.

INT. VISITOR'S CENTER - DAY

An overhead bell JINGLES.

Evelyn enters the Visitor's Center.

Behind the desk:

CLAY BLANCHE -- late 30s, name tag and uniform, moustache
and shaggy hair. Insignia:

"GRASSY GLADE COURTESY PATROL"

Big smile as she enters.

                    CLAY
          Evelyn! So good to see you.

                    EVELYN
          Hello, Clay.

                    CLAY
          You're a little early. Thought you
          were comin' the 4th.

                    EVELYN
          I had to get out of Nashville. If
          you know what I mean.

> CLAY
> Man trouble?

> EVELYN
> No surprise, huh?

> CLAY
> If you want my opinion... he seemed
> liked an asshole.

> EVELYN
> He WAS an asshole.

he signs in.

lay hands her a pass.

> CLAY
> On the dash, same as always. Hey!
> You can come to the party.

> EVELYN
> What party?

> CLAY
> They're throwing me a party for my
> 10-year work anniversary. Tonight
> at the Community Center.

> EVELYN
> They love a good excuse, don't
> they? Not that you're not worth
> it, Clay--

> CLAY
> --You bet I'm worth it!

> EVELYN
> Okay then. See you there.

he exits.

T. LAKE - SHORELINE - DAY

e Tanner Chemical pick-up truck SLAMS to a stop at the
ore of the lake.

rgil hops out.

tices Ralph's fishing rod, dropped on the sand.

Bait box tipped and empty.

No Ralph.

                VIRGIL
     Shoot.

His gaze goes to the water.

The platform, as he left it. Quiet.

Fred Kent -- in work clothes, tired expression -- exits the
passenger side of the truck.

                FRED
     How we gonna get out there?

                VIRGIL
     There's a raft.

Virgil points to the water's edge where, shrouded in shore
plants -- yellow raft with oars.

Virgil retrieves his binoculars. Hands them to Fred.

Fred sights the platform, the Workers.

                FRED
     They're all dead.

                VIRGIL
     Yep.

                FRED
     We're not going out there, are we?

                VIRGIL
          (irritated)
     You want the money, don't you?

                FRED
     But we don't even know what killed
     'em.

Virgil calculates.

                VIRGIL
     The raft carries three. You'll go
     out and back with two each trip.
     Four trips ought to do it--

                    FRED
          --You're not comin' with me?

irgil checks his watch.

                    VIRGIL
          It's 9:15. We need to clear them
          by 10:00.

                    FRED
          What if someone comes by?

                    VIRGIL
          Fred, we picked this part of the
          lake because it's the deepest and
          the quietest. Once the bodies are
          in this truck, we'll put the tarp
          over and drive 'em to base-camp.
          Then we'll call the authorities.

red nods, crosses to the yellow raft. Yanks away the
linging plants. Steps onto the raft, takes the oars.

irgil moves to Ralph's abandoned fishing rod.

icks it up.

cans the shoreline.

eturns to his truck and tosses the rod -- BANG! -- into the
ear bed.

T. ADAMS HOME - KITCHEN - DAY

rpy Adams drinks coffee at her kitchen window.

ots her daughter's Corolla drive onto the property.

                    HARPY
          Jesse! We have a little visitor!

T. ADAMS HOME - DAY

sse and Harpy greet Evelyn in the driveway.

                    HARPY
          Evelyn! What are you doin' here?

elyn hugs her mother.

>   EVELYN
> I hope it's okay that I--

>   JESSE
> --No, no, not a problem, baby girl.
> Are you okay?

Evelyn breaks into tears, hugs her mother. Jesse pats his daughter's back.

>   JESSE (CONT'D)
> Your room's just as you left it.

INT. ADAMS HOME - GUEST ROOM - DAY

Evelyn opens the door to her parents' guest room.

Double-bed, bright colors, stuffed animals, country flair.

Sets down her suitcase.

>   HARPY (O.S.)
> I'll make you some coffee.

>   EVELYN
> Thanks, Mom.

Evelyn sits on the bed. Uncovers a stuffed pet. Hugs it.

>   EVELYN (CONT'D)
>   (to herself)
> Shit, Evelyn. Back one more damn
> time. When are you gonna get your
> shit together?

EXT. LAKE - DAY

Fred oars away from the platform, the bodies of two dead Workers laid out on the yellow raft.

Disgusted, looks sick.

EXT. LAKE - SHORELINE - DAY

Virgil shoves over the foot of a bloodied Worker, makes room for more in the Tanner truck. Four already in the bed.

He yanks the tarp to cover the bodies.

irgil watches Fred row.

hen he looks away--

-SOMETHING catches Virgil's eye.

n weeds down the shoreline...

OOM!

N ARM. Fingers in a grasp!

irgil quick-steps to the spot.

t's the body of Ralph Dorem -- ripped to shreds.

irgil covers his mouth, spins away. Steadies himself.

urns again to the corpse.

e bends. Searches the pockets.

allet. License.

RALPH ESSEX DOREM"

ING! Virgil's cell.

e pockets Ralph's wallet.

> ROY
> (over the phone)
> It's ten o'clock.

> VIRGIL
> We're almost done.

> ROY
> You're late. That marine helping?

> VIRGIL
> Yeah. He'll keep his mouth shut.
> But... there's another body here.
> A fisherman named Ralph Dorem. Mr.
> Alma... I don't think this was an
> accident. I think someone's got it
> out for Tanner. Mr. Alma? Roy?

> ROY
> Bring me Mr. Dorem as well.

ick.

EXT. LAKE - DAY

Fred rows towards shore.

Eyes the water.

Startles!

> FRED
> Holy shit!

A humanoid SHAPE appears under the lake!

Fred SNATCHES the oars out of the water.

Looks to Virgil, dragging Ralph's body to the truck.

> FRED (CONT'D)
> Who's that!

> VIRGIL
> It's nobody! Row! We've got a
> schedule to keep.

SOMETHING jostles the raft!

Fred holds tight.

When it settles, he stares into the water.

Nothing.

Now over the opposite side.

Nothing--

EXT. LAKE - SHORELINE - DAY - SAME MOMENT

--Virgil, eyes to Fred on the raft.

> VIRGIL
> Hurry up!

Fred continues to inspect the water.

> VIRGIL (CONT'D)
> For Christ's sake, Kent--

> FRED
> --Something -- something's in the
> water. I, I saw it!

                    VIRGIL
          We're late. Just get your ass to
          shore.

e watches Fred, who, at last, picks up the oars.

ows. Fast.

reatures SPRING from the water!

wamp the raft.

red TUMBLES OVERBOARD.

he two dead bodies with him.

red SCREAMS as he's pulled under.

appens so quick.

irgil freezes, still holds Ralph's arms in a drag.

tunned, he watches the empty raft float aimlessly.

othing's comes up. Not even bubbles.

irgil snaps out of it.

cops Ralph.

ans to the truck!

rom a mount in cab, he cracks open a long-box.

nside: a high-powered RIFLE with a scope.

irgil winds the strap around his arm.

cks the bolt. Aims at the water.

V:
he gun-sight. The raft.

he gun-sight goes BLACK!

rgil tumbles back.

 Creature -- right in front of him!

 swipes an arm and KNOCKS Virgil to the ground.

e rifle goes off -- BAM-!

SMASH CUT TO:

EXT. WARREN HOUSE - DAY

Herb Warren stands with TINA -- 40s, in nurse uniform --
beside her parked Ford Fiesta in the Warren house driveway.

Virgil's rifle shot echoes across the lake.

                    HERB
          You hear that?

                    TINA
          Must be a hunter.

                    HERB
          There's no hunting in the Glade.
               (beat)
          I'll stop by Resident Services and
          report it. Might be poachers.

Herb climbs into her Ford.

                    HERB (CONT'D)
          Thanks, Tina, for letting me borrow
          your car. And for everything else.
          You're a life saver.

He revs the engine and backs out of the drive as Tina start
towards the Warren house.

EXT. GOLF COURSE - DAY

WHACK!

Don Le Mans knocks a golf ball down the fairway.

Beside him, Jesse Adams, wood driver in hand.

                    DON
          Let's make this game interesting.

Jesse tees up.

                    JESSE
          Not today, Don.

                    DON
          A friendly wager.

                    JESSE
          Last wasn't so friendly. I lost
          $500.

                    DON
          Tell you what, we won't go over
          $100.

on lines up his swing.

                    JESSE
          Money messes with my game.

HACK!

nother drive down the fairway, this one off to the left.

                    JESSE (CONT'D)
          Shit.

XT. GOLF COURSE - DAY - LATER

on and Jesse drive the fairway in a golf cart.

                    JESSE
          ...So she's with us.

                    DON
          That's too bad, Jesse. Evelyn's a
          catch -- she doesn't deserve the
          proletariat.

                    JESSE
          She fell for a country and western
          singer. In Nashville. He'll
          probably write a hit song about
          her.

on stops the cart. The two men dismount.

                    JESSE (CONT'D)
          At least he wasn't Republican.

                    DON
          Ha, ha, hey! Be careful what you
          say. These hills have eyes. And
          ears.

INT. RESIDENT SERVICES - DAY

Herb steps into Grassy Glade Resident Services.

Small office, THREE OLD VOLUNTEERS at desks.

                    HERB
          I'd like to report gunfire.

INT. TANNER CHEMICAL - OFFICE - DAY

Roy Alma hangs up the big phone on his big desk.

Looks to Victoria and Shirley Evans, seated.

Roy huffs, leans in.

                    ROY
          No one's answerin'.
               (beat)
          Maybe I should. Maybe I should...

                    VICTORIA | SHIRLEY
          Should what, Roy?

                    ROY
          ...call the sheriff. He likes
          money as much as the next guy.

                    VICTORIA
          Something wrong, Roy?

                    ROY
          Workers asleep on the job.

Roy lights a pipe.

                    ROY (CONT'D)
          I know, darlins! I'll go down
          there myself. Apply a little
          pressure. How about that, girls?
          You want to visit the heart of
          America one more time?

                    VICTORIA
          Do you want your limo, Roy?

He likes the idea.

                    ROY
          I want my limo. Yes.

                    SHIRLEY
          And your champagne?

                    ROY
          Do you really think, Shirley, that
          this is a time for champagne?

                    SHIRLEY
               (shrugs)
          It could be.

oy stands, circles the desk, places a hand on each woman's
houlder.

                    ROY
          Yes.   Champagne.

                    VICTORIA | SHIRLEY
          Yay!

XT. ACCESS ROAD - DAY

 sheriff's brown and white Dodge Charger kicks up dust on
1 unpaved access road overlooking Salamander Lake.

 a precipice, the Charger stops.

xiting the vehicle...

..SHERIFF RICK HEMSDALE -- 40s, craggy face, sidearm,
)o-tight uniform.

e reaches into his car.   Finds binoculars.

)rth to south, he scans the lake.

)ats.   Midday sun.

.rds and tranquility.

JZZ!

iort wave crackles.

iswers it through the open car window.

                    HEMSDALE
               Go for Rick.

 spatcher -- MATTIE -- on the radio.

                    MATTIE
               (over radio)
          We had a report of rifle fire in
          the Glade.

                    HEMSDALE
          How do you know it was a rifle?

                    MATTIE
          Herb Warren reported it.

                    HEMSDALE
          Well. He would know. When?

                    MATTIE
          'Bout noon.

                    HEMSDALE
          Okay. I didn't hear it, but I'll
          check it out.

Disconnects. Goes back to scanning with his binoculars.

Lands on the shore below.

Virgil Hamlin's Tanner Chemical truck.

No bodies. Tarp covering the bed.

Takes down his binoculars.

Moves to the car radio.

                    HEMSDALE (CONT'D)
          You still there, Mattie?

                    MATTIE
               (over radio)
          Go for Mattie.

                    HEMSDALE
          A Tanner truck is parked at the
          waterline. Can you check for a
          work order? Wanna be right before
          I'm mad as hell.

EXT. LAKE - SHORELINE - DAY

Sheriff Hemsdale traverses the rocky shoreline.

No Virgil. No Ralph.

e now spots the platform in the distance.

hen, the drifting yellow raft.

emsdale lifts his binoculars.

he platform's empty.

                    HEMSDALE
          When it rains it pours.

XT. GOLF COURSE - DAY

esse Adams trails Don Le Mans from a green to their golf
art, iron in hand. Drained, Jesse stuffs the club back
nto his bag and wipes his brow.

                    JESSE
          I should knock off.

                    DON
          It's only the 14th!

                    JESSE
          It's too hot. I don't want to end
          up with a cardiac.

                    DON
          You just want to sip tea with
          Evelyn on your porch.

                    JESSE
          Maybe I do. She's probably up by
          now. You going to Clay's party?

                    DON
          Got a date.

                    JESSE
          Oh?

                    DON
          Peggy Marsh. Ha, ha, hey!

                    JESSE
          I like the body but not the mind.

                    DON
          Who cares about the mind when you
          got the body?

Jesse shakes his head, climbs in the cart.

Don takes a seat behind the wheel.

Don spots:

An ELDERLY GOLFER -- 50 yards off in a sand trap.

>   DON (CONT'D)
>   Look at old Forrester there.   That
>   trap's his damn Waterloo.

The Elderly Golfer takes a swing.   Another.   Cusses.

>   JESSE
>   He better watch it or he's gonna be
>   the one with the heart attack.

>   DON
>   If he wants to die playin' golf,
>   that's his right as an American.

Don revs the cart, drives them off in a direction.

PAN TO REVEAL:

The Elderly Golfer has now... vanished.

EXT. COMMUNITY CENTER - DAY

Don and Jesse arrive at the Community Center, set against
the golf course.

An ATTENDANT greets them, lifts the men's clubs from the
back of the cart, moves to store them.

Nearby, Jimmie Calvin chats up a VALET racking car keys.

>   JIMMIE
>   And you ain't seen Fred?

>   VALET
>   Nope, sorry.

>   JIMMIE
>   But that's his car.

Points to a blue Chevy in the lot.

                    VALET
          Hey, yeah... He mighta been here
          earlier. Some dude picked him up.
          They seemed a little weird, like it
          was a secret.

                    JIMMIE
          A secret? What do you mean?

                    VALET
          I dunno. Just they were talkin'
          quiet.

Jimmie stares at the Chevy, perplexed.

EXT. ADAMS HOME - PORCH - DAY

Evelyn Adams rocks in a chair-swing on the porch of her
parent's house, sips tea in the mid-day sun.

Harpy exits the house, takes the lounge chair.

                    HARPY
          You can stay. Long as you want.

                    EVELYN
          I do like this place.

                    HARPY
          Well, it'll be yours when your
          father and I pass--

                    EVELYN
          --I like you around.

                    HARPY
          I like me around, too!

Evelyn, concerned.

                    EVELYN
          How's dad doing?

                    HARPY
          His cardiologist gave him a clean
          bill.
                    (beat)
          What? He's good, he's good! Don't
          give me that look.

                    EVELYN
          You're not telling me everything.

                    HARPY
          He's playin' golf. What does that
          show you? He's probably already
          lost this month's social security
          to Don Le Mans.

Shared smile.

EXT. LAKE - SHORELINE - DAY

Sheriff Hemsdale beats the brush south of the shore.

Goes further, into a outcropping of woods--

EXT. WOODS - DAY - CONTINUOUS

--Sheriff Hemsdale makes his way through 25 feet of brush.

Squared in the middle, he surveys the tall, dark trees.

SNAP!

Hemsdale turns. Considers.

Keeps moving deeper into the woods.

                    HEMSDALE
          Anyone here?

Silence. He stalls a moment. Then heads back to the trees.

Unseen... a Creature sloughs from around a tree.

Then another. Another.

WIDE SHOT:

There are Creatures next to nearly EVERY tree in the woods.

INT. SHERIFF'S OFFICE - DAY

Mattie the Dispatcher -- 60s, cat-eye glasses and too-large
blouse -- lifts up from a desk stacked with paperwork to
answer the buzz of the radio.

> MATTIE
Go for Mattie.

ROSS-CUT CONVERSATION.

> HEMSDALE
> (over radio)
I got nothin' out here. That work
order turn up?

> MATTIE
Clay doesn't remember one being
placed. But 'cha got a call from
Roy Alma.

> HEMSDALE
Alma? All right, I'll hit the
boat-yard then I'll give him a call
back. Out.

> MATTIE
Don't be too long, Rick. You got
to get ready for Clay Blanche's
party tonight. Out.

> HEMSDALE
No, not 'out,' Mattie. Don't you
think that an abandoned Tanner
Chemical truck and rifle fire are
more important than a party? Over.

> MATTIE
> (sweetly)
But Clay would sure like to see you
there.

> HEMSDALE
Wh-- Fine. I will try. Out.

Mattie returns to her paperwork.

Phone RINGS.

> MATTIE
Sheriff's Department.

A woman's shaky VOICE.

> VOICE
I'd like to report a missing
person.

>   MATTIE
>   Oh no, who?

>   VOICE
>   My husband went out fishing on
>   Salamander Lake this mornin', but
>   he ain't come back. His name is
>   Ralph Dorem.

She writes it down.

>   MATTIE
>   What was he wearin', Mrs. Dorem?

>   VOICE
>   Oh, his vest and that cap he likes.
>   He's 67 and still has hair, kin you
>   believe it?

>   MATTIE
>   Well, that's good.

>   JUMP CUT TO:

INT. WOODS - DAY

Ralph Dorem -- the top of his head taken off in one bite by
a Creature as his body is ravaged in the woods.

INT. RESIDENT SERVICES - DAY

A phone rings at Grassy Glade Resident Services.

A PLUMP WOMAN answers.

>   PLUMP WOMAN
>   Grassy Glade Resident Services.
>   (beat, concern)
>   Oh. Okay. Yes. Thank ya, Mattie.

Hangs up.

An older VOLUNTEER overhears, turns in his chair.

>   VOLUNTEER
>   They say there's some missin'
>   people, and if we hear anything, we
>   should give 'em a call right away.

She stands.

                    PLUMP WOMAN
          I better... I'd better write that
          down--

                    VOLUNTEER
          --I'll remember! Sharp as a tack-!

                    PLUMP WOMAN
          --I'd better write that down.

NT. WARREN HOUSE - KITCHEN - DAY

erb Warren enters his house, struggles with a bag of
roceries.

o one in the kitchen. He sets down the bag.

                    HERB
          Tina!

o answer. Takes out a couple things from the bag. Stops.

anders back into the house.

aiet.

earing the end of the hallway--

-Nurse Tina sits with his wife Linda in the master bedroom.

a Tina's lap, a photo album.

                    TINA
          I didn't hear ye come in. We were
          just lookin' at some pictures.
          Weren't we, Linda?

o response.

.na closes the album, slides out.

                    TINA (CONT'D)
          She's been asking about her mother.
          Thinks she's somewheres in the
          house.

                    HERB
          You mean her DEAD mother.

                    TINA
          Well... So, I thought we'd share
          some pictures. She seemed to enjoy
          it.

                    HERB
          How could you tell?

She touches his arm.

                    TINA
               (softer)
          Messed herself a little. I got her
          cleaned up.
               (beat)
          They help you with those gunshots?

Herb shakes his head.

                    HERB
          Nope. So don't pretend this is
          Chicago and get shot when you
          leave, okay?

She smiles.

                    TINA
          I'll never pretend this place is
          Chicago.

EXT. LAKE - DAY

Sheriff Hemsdale drives his Dodge Charger up an unpaved road
near Salamander Lake.

He sights SOMETHING MOVE, left of the road.

Keeps driving, but reaches for his binoculars.

When he comes up--

--10 feet beyond him, in the road!

BUSTER GILSON -- late 70s, bathrobe and slippers.

Brakes! Buster, as shocked as the sheriff.

Hemsdale takes off his cap, tosses it on the dash.

Puts the Charger in park, steps out.

                    HEMSDALE
          What in the hell you doin' in the
          middle of the damn road, Buster!

                    BUSTER
               (flustered)
          Walkin'.

                    HEMSDALE
          Well, Key-rist almighty, Buster. I
          nearly gave you wings. And
          where're your damn clothes!

ister looks down.

emsdale shakes his head. Grrr.

NT. SHERIFF'S DODGE - MOVING - DAY

heriff Hemsdale drives the Dodge Charger.

ister Cilson in the passenger seat.

                    HEMSDALE
          How you doin' there, Old Timer?

                    BUSTER
          Oh, my hips hurt. And my knees.
          Got to get me some new ones.

                    HEMSDALE
          Then what you doin' out walkin'?

                    BUSTER
          I thought I seen somethin'.

                    HEMSDALE
          What'd you see?

                    BUSTER
          People in my weeds. Big guys with
          big heads.

                    HEMSDALE
          Big heads?

ister makes a size approximation with parenthetical hands.

                    HEMSDALE (CONT'D)
          That's brain damage, Buster.

                    BUSTER
          Alls I'm sayin'... is that they
          gots big heads.

INT. GENERAL STORE - DAY

Evelyn enters the general store.

Leo Barry, behind the counter. Sits up, takes notice.

She smiles at him and heads for beer case.

                    LEO
          Can I help you find somethin',
          Evelyn?

                    EVELYN
          Dad wants to give Clay some beer.
          As a present. Got anything fancy?

Leo comes from around the counter.

                    LEO
          Fancy beer's more Nashville than
          Grassy Glade.

                    EVELYN
          You must have something better than
          Miller Lite.

Leo scans the case.

                    LEO
          Let's see... So you gonna be at
          the party?

                    EVELYN
          I guess so.

                    LEO
          Me, too. I like Clay and I'm
          always up for a party.

                    EVELYN
          It's two hours of people who can't
          hear complaining about their health
          and talkin' politics and God.

                    LEO
          You may be right there. But it
          beats seein' 'em in church.

raws a six-pack from the case.

>   LEO (CONT'D)
>   How 'bout this one?

velyn inspects.

>   EVELYN
>   15 dollars!

>   LEO
>   I'll give you a discount.

>   EVELYN
>   Not necessary. I'm just thinkin'
>   -- this will be perfect, 'cos Clay
>   would never pay that much for six
>   beers.

hey step back to the counter, Leo at the register.

>   LEO
> $16.21.

he pays him. He bags the beer.

>   EVELYN
>   Thanks.

 smile.

>   LEO
>   You're welcome. See you at the
>   party.

>   EVELYN
>   I hope so.

he leaves.

 raises a brow.

T. COMMUNITY CENTER - DAY

mmie Calvin, outside the Community Center.

tes his nails.

 his sights: Fred's blue Chevy.

The Valet returns from parking a car, hangs keys on a nearby
box. Locks it. Notes Jimmie.

> VALET
> You still waitin' fer Mr. Kent?

Jimmie nods.

> VALET (CONT'D)
> It's nearly five o'clock.

> JIMMIE
> I know.

> VALET
> He wouldn't miss the party.

> JIMMIE
> You stayin' for that?

> VALET
> I'm off at six.

Jimmie -- eyes fixed on the Chevy.

EXT. LAKE - PATH - DAY

The sheriff's car rounds the lake path.

INT. SHERIFF'S DODGE - MOVING - DAY - SAME MOMENT

Sheriff Hemsdale drives with Buster Gilson.

Car kicks up road dust. Ahead, brambles, waves of heat.

Buster's finger goes out!

> BUSTER
> There's one of 'em!

POV:
Out the windscreen, a Creature steps into the tall brush.

Hemsdale slows and stops.

> HEMSDALE
> I didn't see nothin'.

> BUSTER
> Right there. Right. There.

                         HEMSDALE
          On the left?

                         BUSTER
          On the left. Went into them weeds.
          Big ol' head.

he Sheriff puts the car in 'park.' Takes out his baton.

teps from the car, leans back in.

                         HEMSDALE
          Don't you drive off now. Hear?

                         BUSTER
          I ain't drove since my daughter hid
          my keys five years ago.

he Sheriff nods, slams the door--

XT. LAKE - PATH - DAY - CONTINUOUS

-On the lake path, Sheriff Hemsdale separates from his
ehicle, slowly walks to the bushes, hand on his baton.

                         HEMSDALE
          This is the Sheriff! Anyone in
          them bushes?

eps walking.

                         HEMSDALE (CONT'D)
          You haven't done nothin' wrong, but
          I am armed and you do not want you
          to get shot for no good reason.

eps walking.

JT. SHERIFF'S DODGE - DAY - CONTINUOUS

ister leans into the dash of the Sheriff's car as Hemsdale
proaches the brush.

                         BUSTER
          Come out, ya big-headed bastard.

NG!

 the passenger side--

--a Creature SMACKS its spidery fingers against the window!

                    BUSTER (CONT'D)
          Oh, Lordy!

Buster rotates.

Three Creatures surround the car.

Two at the side, one at the back.

Eyes ahead to Hemsdale, who beats his baton through the
brambles, oblivious.

                    HEMSDALE
                  (faraway)
          Come out now, ya hear!

Silently, the three Creatures slime all over the car, try t
get inside.

Buster locks the doors!

He HONKS the car horn.

BEEP! BEEP!

EXT. LAKE - PATH - DAY - CONTINUOUS

Sheriff Hemsdale turns.

Sees the Creatures at his car.

                    HEMSDALE
          Ho-lee shit!

He staggers onto the road.

He drops his baton, draws out his gun.

                    HEMSDALE (CONT'D)
          Hey! You!

The Creatures stop. Turn their big ugly heads.

                    HEMSDALE (CONT'D)
          Away from the car!

Standoff.

NT. SHERIFF'S DODGE - DAY - CONTINUOUS

nside the car, Buster panics.

hecks for a weapon.

hotgun beside the driver's seat.

ries to loosen. No good.

hen he looks back up--

-Hemsdale, in the middle of the path.

ehind the sheriff...

..A DOZEN MORE CREATURES...

..that Hemsdale doesn't see.

uster honks the horn. Tries to signal.

oo late!

he Creatures ATTACK Hemsdale on the path-!

XT. LAKE - PATH - DAY - CONTINUOUS

-Hemsdale fights!

e's CLAWED with animal fury.

un GOES OFF! BAM!

he bullet PIERCES the car's windshield -- nearly hits
uster -- leaves a web-like hole in the glass.

emsdale fires three shots into the air! BANG BANG BANG.

ts nothing.

JT. SHERIFF'S DODGE - DAY - CONTINUOUS

rom the passenger seat, Buster swings his leg onto the gas.
lifts to 'drive.'

he Dodge Charger rolls, just as--

-a Creature CRASHES through the rear windshield!

Buster looks ahead--

--Sheriff Hemsdale -- bloody, ravaged, dead.

The dozen attacking Creatures rise up just as--

--Buster SLAMS on the accelerator.

The Creature ROLLS off the trunk.

The car PLOWS THROUGH Creatures, flattens Hemsdale.

Buster attempts to control, to keep the car on the path.

But he can't.

The Charger SLIPS into a gully, tire in mud.

Buster ZOOMS the accelerator. No use. Stuck.

> BUSTER
>> Oh, no.

The Creatures -- coming his direction!

INT. LAKE HOUSE - DAY

Sidney Reed opens his front door to find--

--Roy Alma and the Evans sisters, on his porch, expectant.

> SIDNEY
>> Roy!

> ROY
>> Sid, step aside.

Roy barrels into the house.

> ROY (CONT'D)
>> I can't get Hamlin on the phone, I
>> can't get Rudy Galvan on the phone,
>> No one can even raise the goddamn
>> sheriff. Where the hell were you?

> SIDNEY
>> I was getting ready.

Sidney gestures to his dapper shirt, pressed pants.

                    ROY
        Ready for what?

                    SIDNEY
        There's a party.

                    ROY
        A party, a party. There's always a
        goddamn party in this place.
        You're going with me to the
        platform. We're gonna find out
        where my men are.

                    VICTORIA | SHIRLEY
        But we want to go to a party!

                    ROY
        Soon, darlins.

    dney grabs keys from a hanging post.

                    SIDNEY
        You and me will take my truck.
        Your wheels will never make it down
        the gully.

                    VICTORIA
        Aren't we going to the party?

                    ROY
        We'll have the driver take you.
        Sid and me will take care of a
        little business.

                    SHIRLEY
        What kind of party is it?

                    SIDNEY
        Uh, it's a work anniversary. One
        of the guards.

                    SHIRLEY
        Yay!

                    VICTORIA
        How fun!

    dney shakes his head.

                    ROY
        Sounds boring as shit.

Gestures to the door.

INT. VISITOR'S CENTER - DAY

Clay Blanche watches the clock tick to 5:30.

CHUCK -- 20s, in guard uniform -- enters the Visitor's
Center.

>   CLAY
>   Worried you'd be late.

>   CHUCK
>   And let you miss your party!

>   CLAY
>   It's a stupid idea anyway, Chuck.
>   Ten years of sitting in a shack,
>   letting people in and out of a
>   gate.

>   CHUCK
>   Hey, man, take the free beer when
>   you can, right?

Clay exits with a smirk.

INT. MARSH HOUSE - NIGHT

Peggy Marsh wears a low-cut dress and a perfectly placed
wig. She waits in her living room for--

--a KNOCK on her front door.

She rises to answer.

Don Le Mans, on her stoop. Bow-tie and patched coat.

>   DON
>   You look adorable.

>   PEGGY
>   Thank you.

>   DON
>   Uh... Hmmm. Where's your roommate?

>   PEGGY
>   Mr. Hamlin left this morning. He
>   hasn't come back.

on steps inside.

>   DON
>   Forget him. I don't want a younger
>   man charming my date anyway.

he blushes.

>   PEGGY
>   I was warned about you.

>   DON
>   All rumors are true.

>   PEGGY
>   So where are you taking me?

>   DON
>   I thought about the Castle.

>   PEGGY
>   We're not going to the party?

>   DON
>   I want you all to myself.

>   PEGGY
>   I bet you do.

e gestures.

>   DON
>   My lady, your chariot awaits.

he grabs her purse. Ready.

T. ADAMS HOME - DUSK

elyn Adams descends the stairs of her parents' house.
ars a simple dress.

r mother frowns.

>   EVELYN
>   What?

>   HARPY
>   Is that all you're wearing?

>   EVELYN
>   It's summer.

Jesse enters the room, jacket and neck-tie.

> HARPY
> See? Even your father put on a
> tie.

> EVELYN
> I'm comfortable.

> HARPY
> Leo Barry will be there.

She rolls her eyes.

> EVELYN
> Don't set me up! I'm warning you.
> Not tonight. If there's a move,
> I'm gonna make it on my own.

Gives her mother a kiss on the cheek.

> HARPY
> So you're not going to change?

> EVELYN
> No, Mom. I may not even stay more
> than an hour, so this is fine.

> HARPY
> What should we say when they ask
> why you're here?

> EVELYN
> They won't care.

> JESSE
> The men will care.

> EVELYN
> Tell them I'm pregnant.

> JESSE
> Evelyn!

> EVELYN
> Come on. I'll be nice. Swear.

INT. WARREN HOUSE - DUSK

Nurse Tina readies herself to leave the Warren house.

erb fixes a drink.

inda, catatonic in the corner chair.

> TINA
> Goin' to the party?

> HERB
> I'm tired.

> TINA
> I have to head to Marysville to see
> my sister.

> HERB
> Drive safe. It's gettin' dark.

> TINA
> 'Bye.

> HERB
> 'Night, Tina.

he opens the front door of the house and--

-RIGHT THERE on the stoop.

Creature. Big. Gross.

ina SLAMS the door.

> TINA
> (breathless)
> Oh my.

erb, confused.

ina backs from the door.

> HERB
> What's wrong?

he keeps on backing up.

> HERB (CONT'D)
> (half-laugh)
> What is it?

e raises her finger.

> TINA
> There's-- There's--

He moves to the door.

>   TINA (CONT'D)
>   --Don't open it!

Herb now senses the gravity.

>   HERB
>   Oh, another bear, huh?

He looks through the peep-hole.

Goes white.

Stands back, stunned.

Spins the lock shut.

>   HERB (CONT'D)
>   That's not a bear.

He steps next to Tina.

>   HERB (CONT'D)
>   Make sure all the doors are locked.

She nods, rushes out of the room.

The shadow of the creature glances through the curtained sidelites.

Herb takes one more step back.

Turns his head to Linda.

Then back to the door.

Tina returns.

>   TINA
>   Doors are locked.

>   HERB
>   And the garage?

>   TINA
>   And the garage door is closed.
>   (beat)
>   What is that thing?

Slowly, he shakes his head.

NT. SHERIFF'S OFFICE - DUSK

attie answers the telephone in the Sheriff's office.

> MATTIE
> Sheriff's Department.
> (beat)
> How many you heard? Five or six.
> Okay. Could you tell where they
> were comin' from? No. Okay. Yes.
> Thank ya for reportin' it.
> All-righty now.

he disconnects. Moves to the radio.

> MATTIE (CONT'D)
> Sheriff... You there? Over.
> (beat)
> Calling Sheriff Rick Hemsdale.
> Over.
> (beat)
> We have reports of more gunfire at
> the lake. Over.
> (beat)
> Should I... should I call the state
> police?

JZZ! Another voice across the wire.

EPUTY VIC McCLURE -- 30s, male.

> MCCLURE
> (over radio)
> This is McClure.

> MATTIE
> Oh, Vic. Did you hear that?

> MCCLURE
> Copy. I'll check 'em out.

> MATTIE
> What's yer location?

> MCCLURE
> Two miles down the mountain.

> MATTIE
> Can you stop by the lake and check
> for Rick? He might be on foot.

                        MCCLURE
              Yep, will do. Out.

Mattie, nervous face.

INT. COMMUNITY CENTER - DUSK

Jimmie Calvin enters the Community Center.

Plows past Waiters and an EMPLOYEE, who sets a blown-up
picture of Clay Blanche onto an easel.

Jimmie heads straight for the bar, where a FEMALE TENDER --
40s -- slides bottles of beer into an ice tub.

                        JIMMIE
              You open yet?

                        FEMALE TENDER
              Party doesn't start 'til six.

                        JIMMIE
              Ten for a beer.

                        FEMALE TENDER
              These aren't cold.

                        JIMMIE
              Don't matter.

She shrugs. Exchanges beer for money.

Jimmie drinks.

                        FEMALE TENDER
              Why you rushin' to drink warm beer
              at ball-park prices?

                        JIMMIE
              Because I'm worried.

                        FEMALE TENDER
              Aw, it's only a party.

                        JIMMIE
              You just keep the drinks comin'.

EXT. CASTLE RESTAURANT - DUSK

Don Le Mans and Peggy Marsh arrive at the Castle Restauran

0 CUSTOMERS, tops.

hown to a table, Don pulls the chair for Peggy, who sits.

 middle-aged HOSTESS hands them menus.

                    PEGGY
          I don't come here enough.

                    DON
          It's the Glade -- where else would
          you go?

                    PEGGY
          I like to cook.

                    DON
          Is that your hobby?

                    PEGGY
          One of 'em.

                    DON
          I like games of chance.

                    PEGGY
          I know. I heard about you.

                    DON
          I used to be in Vegas -- first as a
          card player, then, after I had a
          losing streak and needed some
          steady pay, at Caesar's Palace
          dealing blackjack to tourists.
          But... well, it reaches a point
          that no matter how good you are, or
          what the pull is, they don't want
          an old man behind the table. They
          want some young thing.

 very young FEMALE WAITER stops by, fills waters.

                    FEMALE WAITER
          I'll be back to take your order.

e's off.

                    DON
          Thanks for coming out tonight. I
          thought your dance card was filled
          by Sidney Reed.

                    PEGGY
          Sidney? Oh, he's sweet, but--

                    DON
          --The two of you--

                    PEGGY
          --No. No, no, no. Never. Never,
          never.

                    DON
          A strongly stated 'never' is my
          best friend.

INT./EXT. WARREN HOUSE - DUSK

Herb Warren emerges from the bedroom with a Winchester
carbine.

Tina, at the door.

Linda, in her chair.

                    TINA
          Whatcha gonna do?

                    HERB
          I, I want you to open the door,
          and, and let's see what we're up
          against. He won't dare come in if
          he sees this.

Tina timidly approaches the door.

Reaches for the knob.

She THROWS the door open, and SCREAMS!

No Creature.

Herb sticks his nose out. Looks left. Right.

Moves outside of the house.

                    TINA
          Where you goin'!

                    HERB
              Shhh.

                          TINA
                       (softer)
                 Where you goin'?

erb steps onto the grass, Winchester in hand.

cans his lawn. The woods lead up a hill.

ot another house or person in sight.

e jumps.

ear a hedge--

-15 CREATURES. All turn with dead eyes.

erb ZIPS back inside the house. Bolts the door.

ina, panicked.

                          HERB
                 There's a whole mess 'round the
                 hedge.

                          TINA
                 Call for help.

                          HERB
                 Yeah... yeah.

erb moves to the telephone. Sets down his rifle. Dials.

                          HERB (CONT'D)
                       (into phone)
                 Hello, I have an emergency. Herb
                 Warren. 54 Arnold La--

izzled.

ings up. Dials again.

                          HERB (CONT'D)
                 The phone just cut off.

na SCREAMS!

irough the window of the breakfast nook, just beyond the
ass--

two Creatures!

rb raises his gun... but then thinks better of a shot.

                         TINA
          Do we just, just wait for them to
          leave?

                         HERB
          ...Yeah. We wait.

INT. COMMUNITY CENTER - DUSK

The clock of the Community Center: 6:17 PM.

The room is filling with aged PARTYGOERS.

Balloons and festoons decorate.

A line has formed at the bar.

In a corner, Jimmie Calvin drinks.

Enter: Jesse and Harpy Adams, with Evelyn.

Evelyn spots Jimmie, notices his disconnected look.

                         EVELYN
               'Scuse me.

She breaks from her parents and crosses to Jimmie.

                         EVELYN (CONT'D)
               You look like you been tarred and
               feathered.

                         JIMMIE
               Don't you hate change?

                         EVELYN
          ...Yeah. Sometimes.

                         JIMMIE
               A good thing gets goin'. Then,
               then you get a bad feelin'. Like,
               like it's time for a turn. And you
               just buckle in.

                         EVELYN
               That's once a year for me, Jimmie.
               I get through it.

                    JIMMIE
          Yeah, I like that about you.
          You've visit us a lot, and I never
          get sick of you.

                    EVELYN
          The party's been goin' 15 minutes
          and you're flirtin' with--

                    JIMMIE
          --I'm gay.

he raises her brow.

                    EVELYN
          Oh. I didn't realize that.

                    JIMMIE
          Well. These parts. You hide it
          pretty good.

                    EVELYN
          Well I'm a city girl. So I can
          take it.

mmie drinks.

                    JIMMIE
          Fred's cheatin' on me. Took off
          with someone in a truck today and
          hasn't come back. His car's
          outside.

                    EVELYN
          You two-?

                    JIMMIE
          --Don't tell anyone. But we've
          been seein' each other for three
          years.

                    EVELYN
          Wow, that's longer than any
          relationship I've ever been in.
          I'm here because another crashed
          and burned. I'll be joining you in
          drinkin' soon enough.

o Barry from the General Store enters.

essed sorta nice, or at least makes the effort.

Strokes his beard, scans the party.

Evelyn spots him.

> JIMMIE
> You go enjoy the party. But keep
> an eye on me so that I don't go
> tellin' anyone else anything
> stupid.

She zips her lips.

Walks to Leo, greets him with a smile.

INT. CASTLE RESTAURANT - DUSK

Peggy Marsh and Don Le Mans laugh it up at dinner.

> PEGGY
> Why didn't I know you earlier?

> DON
> You were married.

> PEGGY
> Buck died an old crank. But he
> wasn't always that way. I like a
> gentle man. So... I wish I'd known
> you earlier, is all. I might die
> soon and we're just becomin'
> friends.

> DON
> No, my lady, no. We came here to
> live! Grassy Glade is about life.
> Sure, the last part of it. But
> life nevertheless.

> PEGGY
> I'm sick of everyone I like dyin'--

> DON
> --Well look at it this way--

> PEGGY
> --and I like you.

> DON
> Oh. That's good. I like you, too.

Smiles.

>   PEGGY
>   What were you gonna say?

>   DON
>   Uh. Just a second... I remember.

>   PEGGY
>   I'll wait.

>   DON
>   It's coming to me. Oh-!

>   PEGGY
>   --look at it this way--

>   DON
>   --Yes. Look at it this way: if
>   someone dies now, you won't have to
>   wait a lifetime to see them again
>   in Heaven. Only a couple years and
>   boom! Ha, ha, hey!

he's touched.

>   PEGGY
>   That's beautiful.

e grins wide, digs into his food.

rash-!

-Dishes.

on and Peggy spin as--

-Buster Gilson BURSTS into the restaurant, still in his
athrobe.

>   BUSTER
>   Run for your lives!

.ld-eyed, Buster spins to the Customers, the Hostess.

) one moves.

>   BUSTER (CONT'D)
>   D-- Didn' you hear what I said?

on chuckles, goes back to eating.

>   DON
>   Call the nut-house.

SUDDEN CHAOS-!

--Creatures FLOOD into the restaurant. Dozens of them.

They swarm over Buster Gilson -- RIP him apart.

Creatures SNATCH Customers and Waitresses -- snap necks, drink their blood.

Don and Peggy LEAP to their feet.

>   PEGGY
>   Wh-- Who-- Who is that???

>   DON
>   I don't know! But they're really
>   fucking mad!

MORE CREATURES pour into the restaurant.

Don pulls Peggy into his arms.

Backs to a wall. Helpless. Trapped.

A look between them. They shut their eyes.

In seconds, the Creatures are on them.

INT. WARREN HOUSE - BASEMENT - DUSK

Herb Warren races down the stairs of his house, into his basement. Flicks on the light.

GUNS ENCASED IN PROTECTIVE GLASS line the walls of the basement -- a man cave, yes, but also a mini-armory. He's collector. Big time.

Sets down the Winchester.

Unlocks the case with a key on his belt.

Grabs--

--A PUMP-ACTION SHOTGUN. A REVOLVER. SHELLS AND BULLETS.

Loads the revolver, then the shotgun.

Heads back upstairs, but turns.

Grabs a SECOND SHOTGUN. Loads it.

NT. WARREN HOUSE - DUSK

erb spills out of the basement and rushes to Tina, who
tares at the window at three intimidating Creatures.

e forces the revolver into her hand.

                    TINA
          I don't know how to shoot.

                    HERB
          Point. Pull the trigger. Hope you
          hit something. You got 9 shots.

e readies a shotgun.

                    HERB (CONT'D)
          You're gonna have to try and make
          it to your car.

                    TINA
          What!

                    HERB
          It's in the driveway. They're not
          near it. You have to get help.

                    TINA
          I'm not leavin'!

                    HERB
          Tina, I'm not as fast as you. And
          I have to stay with Linda.

nda, in the chair, drooling.

na stalls.

                    TINA
          What if... what if--

                    HERB
          --Shoot 'em. Don't ask. Shoot
          'em. I, I don't know what these
          things are, but I can spot the
          enemy when I see 'em. I didn't
          vote to put immigrant kids in cages
          because I'm stupid.

e two turn, gaze out the open window.

eatures line the window.

                    TINA
          Can, can they get in?

                    HERB
          They look strong enough.

                    TINA
          So they--

                    HERB
          --They'll get in. Unless you go
          and get us some help.

INT. GRASSY GLADE - COMMUNITY CENTER - DUSK

Victoria and Shirley Evans enter the Community Center.   The
place is hopping, with about 50 Partygoers for Clay
Blanche's anniversary.

The sisters are spotted by Evelyn, who chats up Leo.

                    EVELYN
          Look.

Leo nods. Interesting.

Evelyn shoots a look at her father, who has also noticed th
sisters.

                    JESSE
          What're they doin' here?

Harpy, beside him, cranes her neck.

                    HARPY
          Roy Alma must be in town.

She sips her wine.

The Evans sisters are swept into conversations, out of
sight.

Jesse and Harpy shrug then look upon their daughter, with
Leo. Satisfied look. This is working.

EXT. LAKE - SHORELINE - DUSK

The sun has nearly set.

Sidney Reed stands between his truck and Virgil Hamlin's.

oy Alma surveys the water's edge, tries to see the detail
f the drill platform. In the dim light, he can't.

idney spots Virgil's rifle in the weeds.

e picks it up, slides it in the front seat of the Tanner
ruck.

                    ROY
          What kind of place you runnin'
          here, Sid?

                    SIDNEY
          What kind of company YOU runnin'?
          And, for the record, it's Sidney.

                    ROY
          What?

                    SIDNEY
          You always call me Sid. But my
          name's Sidney.

                    ROY
          What's the damn difference?

                    SIDNEY
          One's not the way I like it.

idney WHIPS the tarp off the back of Hamlin's truck.

e rear bed -- empty, no bodies.

                    SIDNEY (CONT'D)
          I don't like the way you talk to
          me. I gave you this lake. I gave
          you these people! You wouldn't
          have any of this if I--

                    ROY
          --Oh, shut up, you old windbag.
          You wanna turn out your pockets and
          hand over all the money I gave you?
          You've made 10 times more than the
          next man. So don't go thinkin' you
          did this out of Christian charity.

y picks up a rock, throws it at the platform in
ustration.

                    ROY (CONT'D)
          Where are my men! And your
          sheriff. And his deputies. This
          place is like a goddamn graveyard.

Sidney steps from the truck.

                    SIDNEY
          What were they looking for, Roy?
          Eh? You don't need a drill for
          algae.

                    ROY
          You didn't really think this was
          about algae, did you? We developed
          that chemical years ago and held it
          from you 'cos you could never
          afford it. The algae was just a
          bluff.

                    SIDNEY
          What's under there? What's under
          that lake?

                    ROY
          Oil, Sid-NEY. While you've been
          trying to get up the terry-cloth
          skirt of every granny in Grassy
          Glade, I've been buyin' up the
          mineral rights to Salamander Lake.

                    SIDNEY
          What did I sign? Tell me, what did
          I sign!

                    ROY
          You might wanna hire a better
          lawyer. You, you think you know
          these people? This town? Well
          there're 10 towns just like it
          within a day's drive. And they're
          all a bunch of dumb and greedy
          fuckers who hate dark skin, love
          money, and vote against their own
          self-interest.

Sidney takes a SWING at Roy, but Roy easily ducks it.

Dares him to try again.

Another SWING and a miss. Gets tired.

                    ROY (CONT'D)
          You gonna tell these people how
          much I paid? They'll ride you out
          of town on a rail. Me -- they know
          who I am, what I control. They're
          afraid of real power. But they're
          not afraid of you, Sid. In fact,
          my guess is that they all secretly
          hate your guts.

idney POPS Roy on the mouth.

                    ROY (CONT'D)
          How about that? You've got some
          fight left in you. Good. I won't
          feel bad about kicking your ass to
          Kentucky.

by comes at him for a brawl, but--

-Stops. Points behind Sidney.

                    ROY (CONT'D)
          What's that?

dney, fists raised, bobbing and weaving.

                    SIDNEY
          You really do think I'm dumb, don't
          you?

                    ROY
          No -- look behind you!

ehind Sidney, Creatures rise from the water of the lake.

by backs to the truck.

dney holds his stance, but then, at last--

-quickly glances over his shoulder.

                    SIDNEY
          Oh, shit!

 hot steps away from the ugly Creatures moving from the
ter, dripping, covered in plant-life.

 dney scrambles between the two trucks, next to Roy.

                    ROY
          What in the name of the Lord..?

                         SIDNEY
              They look pissed.

                         ROY
              Quick! In the truck!

Both men jump into Sidney's truck, Sidney at the wheel.

Starts the engine.

Ahead on the road -- more Creatures. A whole army.

                         SIDNEY
              How many of 'em are there!

                         ROY
              Just go! Go!

Sidney SLAMS the gas.

The truck RAMS into the first line of Creatures.

Black goo explodes all over the hood.

Roy locks his door.

Sidney locks his, too.

But the truck. It's stuck on the bodies.

They wait, watch as more Creatures emerge.

                         ROY (CONT'D)
              Do you have a gun?

Sidney shakes his head.

                         SIDNEY
              Wait! There was a rifle. I threw
              it in Hamlin's truck.

They both look. The Tanner truck -- swarmed by creatures.

                         SIDNEY (CONT'D)
              I don't want to die this way! I
              thought it'd be cancer. I say,
              God, please let it be cancer--

                         ROY
              --Get your head together!

Roy searches the cab of the truck. Comes up empty.

idney shakes his head.

> SIDNEY
> In the bed of my truck. A nail
> gun. And wood. We can use the
> planks as bats, and, and--

> ROY
> --All right, yes, yes.

oth eye the rear of the cab, the window to the bed.

> ROY (CONT'D)
> How do we get back there?

Creature smacks wet, spidery hands on the driver's side
indow.

idney JUMPS, slams his foot on the accelerator. Top speed.
ut the wheels just spin.

> SIDNEY
> Shit, shit, shit!

ets an idea.

> SIDNEY (CONT'D)
> Ha, ha! Ah!

> ROY
> What?

> SIDNEY
> I'm not so dumb, Roy.

> ROY
> What!

> SIDNEY
> We're on an incline.

e truck, slightly raised on the dirt road.

dney slips the truck into neutral.

oooowly, the vehicle glides backwards down the incline,
ips off the dead Creatures.

hind them, Creatures part like a sea as the truck picks up
eed.

                    ROY
          Ha, ha! Look at that!

                    SIDNEY
          Not so dumb, right?

                    ROY
          Not so dumb!

SPLASH!

The truck hits Salamander Lake.

                    SIDNEY
          Oh, shit.

Sidney once more hits the gas.

Too late! The wheels can't catch on the slippery rocks and
silt. They've slid too far down.

The heavy truck dips below the waterline.

Roy and Sidney's feet -- swamped by lake water.

The truck continues to roll backwards until--

--it free-floats in the lake.

Takes on water in the rear bed.

The nail gun and the boards float away.

                    ROY
          No!

Out of balance, the truck TIPS over.

Roy opens his door to a GUSH of water.

The entire cab spins.

Roy floats out of the truck's cab.

Sidney grabs the wheel, tries to hold on.

                    SIDNEY
          I can't swim!

                    ROY
          You asshole! It's not that deep!

oy, soaked, starts slogging to shore.

ut--

ll around him--

reatures RISE from the water.

hey SNARE his feet! Drag him under. Dead.

ast survivor Sidney SCREAMS!

an't stop screaming!

he truck flips further. Going under fast.

ot gonna make it.

idney holds his breath.

lly under, he opens his eyes.

1 the muck of the lake, the watery darkness, he sees almost
othing. Except...

..one shape. An angry Creature, swimming his way.

idney screams underwater!

XT./INT. WARREN HOUSE - DUSK

urse Tina on the porch of the Warren house.

er car in the driveway. The lawn. No Creatures.

erb stands behind her in the doorway.

e forces her forward with a look.

en she moves off the porch, Herb shuts the door.

OUND: the lock.

na goes white.

oks left. Right. No sign.

na RUNS towards her car -- an awkward waddle.

de of the house! There. They've seen her.

She TRIPS over a garden gnome.

Lands on the grass.

Her revolver FIRES a shot, right into her stomach.

She YELLS OUT in pain-!

--Herb, at the windows.

> HERB
> Get up!

Tina, doubled over, covered in blood, makes it to her feet.

Her keys SLIP from her blood-covered hand.

Jangle on the driveway.

Creatures -- close.

Herb's distant yell:

> HERB (O.S.) (CONT'D)
> Run!

She bends for her keys. Intense pain, nearly passes out.

Creatures a few feet away.

BANG! BANG!

She shoots -- misses one, hits one. They go down in a oily explosions.

She falls against her car.

Opens the driver side door, but--

--doesn't make it.

The Creatures feast upon her.

Herb watches Tina's decimation. Can't look away.

INT. COMMUNITY CENTER - DUSK

At Clay Blanche's party...

...the Evans sisters have taken the stage.

hey sing a country song to an admiring crowd.

t's a potential Oscar nominee for Best Original Song in a
otion Picture.

hen finished -- rousing APPLAUSE, which morphs into a call
or Clay Blanche to take the stage.

                    PARTYGOERS
          Speech!   Speech!

lay acquiesces, makes his way.

t the mic, flanked by the sisters, Clay speaks shyly.

                    CLAY
          Thank you.   All of you.   Really.
          10 years.   Wow.   Goes by so fast.

                    JESSE
               (peanut gallery)
          You're telling us!

aughs.

                    CLAY
          I want you all to know this means a
          lot to me.   I, I'd do anything for
          you people.   You're good people.
          For a Texas boy, you've made me
          feel real welcome.   So... with
          that... Okay.   I'm done.   Enjoy
          your night!

re applause.

T. WARREN HOUSE - NIGHT

rb Warren paces in his house, panicked.

oks out the darkened windows.

's surrounded.

ips his shotguns, sweats like a damp rag.

last, he moves Linda, catatonic in the corner, sets his
apons against a wall.   Kneels.

eaks tenderly, but this is tough.

                    HERB
          Linda. Lovely. I know that you,
          you can't really understand what's
          happening. But, it's bad. I must
          be goin' nuts. I don't think we
          coulda guessed this for you and me.
          After 50 years. 50 years. Jesus.
          I don't know what these monsters
          are, but they, they want to hurt
          us.

Linda gazes blankly.

He kisses her.

                    HERB (CONT'D)
          When you, you think it can't get
          any more horrible... You... You...
          Oh, Linda. I loved you. Once. I
          loved you. But... maybe... Maybe
          it's time.

He trails off, face goes blank.

Using one shotgun as a prop, he stands.

Bends. Kisses his wife again.

Lays the second shotgun at her feet.

Distraught.

                    HERB (CONT'D)
          I'm so fucking sorry, my lovely.
                  (beat)
          Maybe you'll snap out of it. If
          you do, use the shotgun. Just like
          I taught you.

He can hardly keep himself together as he turns off all the
lights in the house. All except one. The lamp next to
Linda.

From the hallway, he blows a kiss.

Then. He opens the front door. Leaves it wide.

Moves to the garage door--

NT. WARREN HOUSE - GARAGE - NIGHT - CONTINUOUS

-Herb, with shotgun, enters the garage.

it by moonlight through a transom.

nside: a Chevy Malibu on blocks, no tires.

erb locks the inner door to the house with a key from his
elt.

e opens the Malibu's door, drops into the backseat.

ocks himself inside the car.

ays in the rear seat. Cradles his gun. Weeps.

XT. WARREN HOUSE - NIGHT - CONTINUOUS

ne open door to the Warren house.

ne single lamp, spotlighting Linda Warren.

t draws the Creatures like moths.

JT. WARREN HOUSE - NIGHT - CONTINUOUS

reatures swarm the house, on a hunt.

nda, in her chair, looks up.

r a split second, she snaps out of her dementia.

                    LINDA
          Oh, my.

 time for the shotgun.

T. WARREN HOUSE - GARAGE - NIGHT - SAME MOMENT

rb Warren, frozen. Hears no screams from Linda.

T. COMMUNITY CENTER - NIGHT

e party for Clay Blanche continues.

sic, drinks, voices.

EXT. COMMUNITY CENTER - PORTICO - NIGHT

Evelyn exits the Community Center, takes-in air on the rear portico. Pulls cigarettes from her purse, lights one.

When she turns, she startles!

                    LEO
          Oh, jeez! Sorry, Evelyn.

Leo Barry, beside her.

                    EVELYN
          You scared me.
               (re: cigarette)
          Don't tell my folks, okay?

                    LEO
          Scouts honor. And I was actually a
          Boy Scout, so you can take that to
          the bank.

                    EVELYN
          It's so loud in there. Everyone
          must have their hearing aids out.

The two look onto the golf course, empty and dark.

                    LEO
          Do you think you'll stay?

                    EVELYN
          Oh, I dunno. Maybe a week or so.
          Catch my breath.

                    LEO
          If I asked you out, would you say
          yes?

                    EVELYN
          Hmmm. First of all, that's a
          terrible way to be asked, 'cos it's
          not really asking.

                    LEO
          Heh, yes, well. Let me try again.
          While you're here, would you like
          to go on a date? With me. I mean,
          just to pass the time.

                    EVELYN
        You don't need to qualify it. Are
        you gonna take me to the Castle
        Restaurant?

                    LEO
        We can leave the Glade, if you
        want. I know a place.

                    EVELYN
        I'll think about it.

he smiles.

                    LEO
        Think about it.

                    EVELYN
        I will.
                (beat)
        Okay. I've thought about it. Yes.
        But during the day. I want to see
        your hands at all times.

                    LEO
        You don't trust me?

                    EVELYN
        No. I don't trust men anymore.

                    LEO
        Fair enough.

mmie Calvin stumbles outside.

                    JIMMIE
        Am I interruptin'?

                    LEO | EVELYN
        No.

                    JIMMIE
        I've been gettin' an earful of
        half-assed conspiracy theories and
        country medicine.

                    LEO
        I hope when I'm that age I don't
        talk about my health.

> EVELYN
> You will. We all will. And we'll
> probably fall for those same stupid
> conspiracies.

Jimmie spots SOMEONE on one of the nearby greens.

> JIMMIE
> Who's that out there?

Evelyn and Leo notice the silhouette.

> LEO
> Can't tell.

> EVELYN
> He's got friends.

She points. A few more silhouettes emerge.

Though they can't tell the detail... it's the Creatures.

A cluster of them. Just standing there.

> JIMMIE
> Hey you! Come on in, join the
> party!

No response.

Evelyn turns away.

> EVELYN
> More deaf people. Anyway, I guess
> I should go back inside. My
> parents will think I abandoned
> ship.

> LEO
> I'll take you back.

> EVELYN
> Such a gentleman.

> JIMMIE
> 'Bye.

Jimmie, alone outside, sways with drink.

Tries to get a better look at the cluster.

Can't make them out.

ut their heads are big.

e moves off the portico.

> JIMMIE (CONT'D)
> Fred? That you, Fred?

ANG!

immie startles at the SMACK of the door.

a OLD MAN -- 70s, skinny, bald -- joins Jimmie.

> OLD MAN
> Beautiful night.

> JIMMIE
> Shore is. Hey, you see those guys?

>ints.

> OLD MAN
> Yep.

> JIMMIE
> Know 'em?

> OLD MAN
> My eyes aren't too good. But they
> shouldn't be just standin' on the
> green like that in a huddle.
> Weight could do some damage. I'll
> go tell 'em.

e Old Man steps off the portico, moves on the cluster.

mmie watches as the Old Man gets halfway across the lawn,
en he abruptly--

stops.

e Old Man speaks -- words don't make it all the way back
Jimmie, who strains to listen.

e Old Man turns and RUNS!

t he's slow. The cluster fans out from the green.

e Creatures have a target.

mmie perks up.

                    JIMMIE
          Hey, you okay?

                    OLD MAN
          Get inside!

Creatures catch him -- bring him to the grass.

Jimmie races off the portico steps to help.

He brakes!

Creatures tear off the Old Man's limbs.

In shock, Jimmie rears back in horror.

He flees to the Community Center--

INT. COMMUNITY CENTER - NIGHT - CONTINUOUS

--Jimmie CRASHES through the door.

Drags a chair to block the portico door.

Then grabs a TABLE and, not caring that PARTYGOERS are
seated at it, pulls a second one to the door.

                    JIMMIE
          Barricade the door! Do it!

Everyone GASPS in horror!

Evelyn, seated with her parents, sees this.

                    EVELYN
          Oh, shit. Drunk alert.

She gets up, hops to Jimmie at the door.

                    EVELYN (CONT'D)
          Jimmie, Jimmie--

                    JIMMIE
          --There's, they, it's--

                    EVELYN
          --Jimmie, Please. You're drunk.
          Come on. Stop. Stop.

Jimmie continues to pile chairs at the door.

                    JIMMIE
          Outside-- They.   This old guy.
          And, and, on the-- They're coming
          this way!

                    EVELYN
          Jimmie.   Slow down.

he Female Tender at the bar SCREAMS!

ll eyes look to her.

reatures -- outside the vista window!

he Female Tender reverses, knocks bottles from the bar.

esse stands.

lay, flustered.

OOM!

he barricade erected by Jimmie takes a hit.

nstinctively, the Partygoers YOWL with each sound.

esse moves to help.

                    HARPY
          Jesse!

                    JESSE
          It's okay.   It's okay.

esse and Jimmie throw their weight against the barricade as
 takes another hit.

elyn, flummoxed.   Snaps out of it.

                    EVELYN
          Get more chairs!

he Partygoers don't move.

OTHER HIT.

                    EVELYN (CONT'D)
          GET MORE CHAIRS!

ay jumps from the stage.

few of the more capable rush to help.

A second barricade starts at the front door.

> EVELYN (CONT'D)
> (to Jimmie)
> What is it? What is it!

> JIMMIE
> I don't know. They... they killed
> someone outside.

A old SKINNY WOMAN screams!

> SKINNY WOMAN
> Immigrants!

> JESSE
> Call the police!

A well-dressed WOMAN IN PINK -- 60s -- moves towards a
telephone on the wall. Grabs the receiver. Listens.

> WOMAN IN PINK
> What's wrong with the phones!

A feeble MAN IN SUIT -- 80s -- takes the phone from her and
listens. Clicks the receiver.

> MAN IN SUIT
> Anyone got a, a--

> EVELYN
> --Cell phone!

Evelyn moves from the barricade as the Blonde Waiter takes
her place.

Lights up her phone. No bars.

> EVELYN (CONT'D)
> These fucking mountains! Does
> anyone have a cell phone?

Blank stares.

> EVELYN (CONT'D)
> No one has a cell phone?

A FRAIL WOMAN raises a hand.

> FRAIL WOMAN
> I have one my grandson bought me
> but I don't know how to work it.

                    FEMALE TENDER
          I have one.

he looks at her phone.

                    FEMALE TENDER (CONT'D)
            No signal.

NOTHER HIT!

 WAVE OF SCREAMS through the room.

artygoers face the open windows.

 FAT MAN wobbles against the bar.

                    FAT MAN
          What are they?

                    FEMALE TENDER
          They have these crazy big heads!

                    FAT MAN
          They -- they're covered in--

                    JESSE
          --They're from the lake!

eople turn to look at Jesse. Consider.

                    FAT MAN
          How do you know?

                    JESSE
          Because of Tanner Fucking Chemical!

JT. WARREN HOUSE - GARAGE - NIGHT

erb Warren, in the back seat of the Malibu, in the dark
arage. Shotgun cradled, he weeps, stifles the sound.

 long moment passes.

IIIIRRRR!

e overhead garage light COMES ON!

e main door starts to lift open.

rb braces, ready to die. Then.

                    MCCLURE (O.S.)
        Hello? Anyone home? Anyone hurt?

Herb springs up from the backseat.

Deputy McClure JUMPS!

                    MCCLURE (CONT'D)
        Shit! Herb, that you?

He nods.

                    MCCLURE (CONT'D)
        What the hell you doin' in the back
        of your car?

Herb, though windows:

                    HERB
            (urgent, soft)
        Go! They're, they're in the house.

                    MCCLURE
        You know your front door is open?
        Seemed strange so I grabbed this
        here remote out of that Fiesta.
            (beat)
        Who'd you say was in the house?

                    HERB
        Monsters.

                    MCCLURE
        Monsters?

McClure comes around the car. Pulls on the door. Locked.

                    MCCLURE (CONT'D)
        Let me in, Herb.

                    HERB
        I can't do that, Vic.

McClure sees the shotgun.

                    MCCLURE
        You got a weapon in there?

                    HERB
        Of course I do.

                    MCCLURE
          Well, don't shoot anybody. Okay?
          We got your call.

                    HERB
          My call?

                    MCCLURE
          Your phone call. It cut off, but
          Mattie heard enough to know it was
          you.

                    HERB
          They got to the phones.

                    MCCLURE
          Who?

                    HERB
          The monsters!

eputy McClure rolls his eyes.

                    MCCLURE
          Is Linda in the house?

                    HERB
          ...Yes.

                    MCCLURE
          I'm gonna have a look--

                    HERB
          --No! Don't go in there.

                    MCCLURE
          Now, Herb. I gotta look and make
          sure she's all right.

Clure draws his service revolver.

ves to the inside door. Tries the knob.

                    HERB
          It's locked.

                    MCCLURE
          I know. You got your key?

rb shakes his head.

                    HERB
          You can't have it.

                    MCCLURE
          I've had a shit day, Herb. Give me
          the goddamn key or I'll arrest you
          for refusin' to comply with a
          direct order.

Herb opens the window a crack. Hands over his house key.

McClure nods a sarcastic thank you. Unlocks the door.

Moves inside the house.

Herb shifts, tries to get a look. Lights on, but sees
nothing more.

Waits a long time.

At last, McClure emerges. A sorrowful face.

He comes around to Herb in the Malibu.

                    HERB
          Did you see?

                    MCCLURE
          I saw.

                    HERB
          Why didn't you shoot them?

                    MCCLURE
          Herb, there are no monsters. But
          Linda... Oh, Christ, Herb. This is
          bad.
                    (beat)
          Open up. I need your weapon.
          Herb.

                    HERB
          Did you-? Did you see the, the
          body by the car? Tina.

McClure glances back down the driveway.

Blood-stain.

                    MCCLURE
          Oh, Herb, what didja do?

                    HERB
          I didn't do anything! It was the
          monsters!

cClure shakes his head.

                    MCCLURE
          Come on. Out--

                    HERB
          --The monsters-!

                    MCCLURE
          --There are no monsters, Herb! Now
          get the fuck out of the car so I
          can call this in!

t last, Herb unlocks.

cClure helps Herb get out.

onfiscates his shotgun. Pumps out the bullets.

                    HERB
          Don't do that! They may still be
          around.

he deputy's face: unperturbed.

                    MCCLURE
          That way.

estures out of the garage--

T. WARREN HOUSE - NIGHT - CONTINUOUS

Herb and Deputy McClure exit the garage.

erb nervously checks the lawn.

he two pass Tina's open car door.

oodstains, no body.

rked further down the drive...

.the deputy's 4x4 Tahoe.

Clure spins Herb around. Cuffs him.

                    HERB
          Wh-- What are you doing?

                    MCCLURE
          You're safer like this.

                    HERB
          What, but--

                    MCCLURE
          --Ye killed your wife, Herb!
          She's. Jesus. To do that to a
          woman you been married to for 50
          years.

                    HERB
          I, I--

                    MCCLURE
          --I know she was a burden, but you
          can't just kill 'er.

                    HERB
          I didn't! I didn't!

Herb, inconsolable.

                    HERB (CONT'D)
          Maybe I did... Maybe I did...

                    MCCLURE
          You don't have to say a thing,
          Herb. I haven't even read you your
          Rights yet.

                    HERB
          I killed her. I did. I left the
          door open. I, oh, God, I, I, I.

                    MCCLURE
          Stop talkin', Herb! Jesus.

Herb crumbles like a baby.

                    MCCLURE (CONT'D)
          Get in the car.

McClure opens the rear door of his vehicle, stuffs Herb
inside. When he comes around the side-!

--Creatures!

pack of them.

cClure almost trips backwards.

>   MCCLURE (CONT'D)
>   What the fuck!

>   HERB
>   Monsters!

eputy McClure's head is RIPPED OFF by a Creature and tossed
nto the 4x4's hood.

erb slams the car door just as it's SPLATTERED with red.

urls his body over the front seat.

eys in the ignition.

till cuffed, he knocks into reverse, hits the gas'

OOM!

e's off down the road.

NT. 4X4 - MOVING - NIGHT - MOMENTS LATER

erb speeds down a winding hillside.

is age, the handcuffs, his panic--

-all combine for a rocky drive.

T. CASTLE RESTAURANT - NIGHT - MOMENTS LATER

erb arrives at the first site on the road:

e Castle Restaurant.

e door is wide open. Lot full of parked cars.

e 4x4 FLIES into the lot--

SMASHES into the bumper of a Lincoln.

rb squirms from the vehicle, huffs towards the restaurant.

INT. CASTLE RESTAURANT - NIGHT

Herb enters the Castle Restaurant.

Stops sudden!

Sees the remains of the slaughter.

The room, the walls, coated with blood.

Bodies everywhere.

Herb throws up.

                    HERB
          My God. My God... My God...

EXT. CASTLE RESTAURANT - NIGHT

Herb returns to the 4x4. Gets in.

Reverses and RIPS the bumper off the Lincoln as he screeche
back onto the road and drives off at a high rate of speed.

INT. COMMUNITY CENTER - NIGHT

Partygoers barricade every vulnerable door and window in th
Community Center.

Clay stops a last square from being covered by chairs.

                    CLAY
          Leave it, leave it! We have to be
          able to see them.

                    HARPY
          How will we get out?

                    FAT MAN
          Who wants to get out? I'm not
          going out. Not with--

                    JESSE
          --She means if they get in.

                    FEMALE TENDER
          They look like, like spacemen.

                    JESSE
          I tell ya, they're from the lake.
          They look like fish--

                    JIMMIE
          --Really fucked up fish--

                    JESSE
          --They have scales and, and,
          something about them... you can
          just tell. Are any of you
          fisherman?

                    FAT MAN
          I'm a fisherman, but I didn't get a
          good look at 'em.

                    JESSE
          They're from the lake!

                    HARPY
          Jesse, calm down!

                    CLAY
          Does it matter? They're here.

esse tosses a last chair on the pile.

                    JESSE
          But if they're from the lake, then
          that means they may have trouble
          breathing. We just have to wait.
          They'll go back to the water!

esse COLLAPSES in pain.

rpy RUSHES to his side.

                    HARPY
              Jesse!

 stampede forward.

                    CLAY
          Back, back, give him air.

rpy loosens her husband's neck-tie.

                    HARPY
          It's his heart.

                    JIMMIE
          Jesus Christ, what next?

                    JESSE
          I'll be okay. Just. Just. Just
          give me a minute.

The faces of the Partygoers. Off the deep end. Distressed

A TALL OLDER WOMAN -- late 50s -- comes forward.

                    TALL OLDER WOMAN
          How many are there? There's dozens
          of us. Maybe we could--

                    JIMMIE
          --I saw at least 10. And, and
          they're kinda slow, but not
          molasses. They'll get you. Can
          any of you run? Like really run
          fast?

Shakes of the head. They're old.

At last, Evelyn raises her hand. Then Jimmie. Then Clay.
Then the Female Tender, the Blonde Waiter, and Leo.

                    CLAY
          Well, if it comes to it, the six of
          us will make a break. Find help.
          But... right now. Let's. Just.
          Wait.

INT. VISITOR'S CENTER - NIGHT

Chuck, at the Visitor's Center, nodding off.

He is awoken by--

--BOOM! CRASH!

The 4x4's mid-speed COLLIDES with the gate!

Chuck springs into action, exits to find--

EXT. VISITOR'S CENTER - NIGHT - CONTINUOUS

--the 4x4, its front flattened, steam rising from the hood

Herb Warren behind the wheel.

huck rushes to the door, pulls out Herb, notices the
andcuffs.

                    CHUCK
          Mr. Warren?

                    HERB
          Please help me.

                    CHUCK
          What the hell? Are you okay?

huck helps Herb from the 4x4.

                    HERB
          You have to believe me. You have
          to. We may not live if you don't
          believe me.

                    CHUCK
          ...Okay.

                    HERB
          We're under attack.

                    CHUCK
          Attack?

                    HERB
          By monsters. They've killed
          everyone at the Castle. And the
          deputy. And Tina... and Linda...

e breaks down at his wife's name.

uck takes his arm, guides him inside the Visitor Center--

JT. VISITOR'S CENTER - NIGHT - CONTINUOUS

Chuck sets Herb in a chair just inside the open door.

                    HERB
          Lock the door.

                    CHUCK
          What?

                    HERB
          Lock it!

uck bolts the door.

Then moves to the telephone.

Picks up the receiver. Makes a face.

> HERB (CONT'D)
> They got the lines. Maybe on
> purpose, maybe by accident.

Chuck takes out his cell phone. Dials.

> HERB (CONT'D)
> Is it working?

> CHUCK
> Yes.

> HERB
> (didn't hear)
> Is it working-?

> CHUCK
> --Yes! Shhh.

Answer on the line.

> CHUCK (CONT'D)
> Yeah, it's Chuck Turkel from Grassy
> Glade. I like to report... an
> emergency.

> HERB
> Did they answer-?

> CHUCK
> --Shhh!
> (into phone)
> Look, I don't know what's going on,
> but I've got a report that people
> might be hurt at the Castle
> Restaurant... Unknown... Unknown.
> Okay, yes, on a short wave. I can,
> yeah. Right now.

He hangs up.

> HERB
> Who was that?

> CHUCK
> Highway Patrol.

> HERB
> They won't be here for an hour!

huck moves to open the door.

> HERB (CONT'D)
> Where are you going?

> CHUCK
> The car. I'll get a quicker
> response from the sheriff if I use
> the radio.

> HERB
> Don't go out there!

> CHUCK
> I have to.

> HERB
> You got a gun?

> CHUCK
> Hell no, you know that.

> HERB
> Take-- take that.

gestures.

> CHUCK
> The coat rack? You gotta be
> kiddin'.

> HERB
> Use it like a, like a spear.

uck hesitates. Opens the door.

rb pleads with his eyes.

last, Chuck smirks, lifts a couple jackets off the cheap
tal coat rack, and takes it outside with him--

T. VISITOR'S CENTER - NIGHT - CONTINUOUS

Chuck descends the steps of the Visitor's Center to the
ashed 4x4.

sets the coat rack against the driver's side door.

Slips inside.

Unhooks the radio.

>   CHUCK
>   Dispatch? Can you hear me?

>   MATTIE
>   (over radio)
>   This is Dispatch. That you, Vic?

>   CHUCK
>   No. It's Chuck. At the Visitor's
>   Center. I... I think we have a
>   problem.

INT. COMMUNITY CENTER - NIGHT

The front door of the Community Center SHUDDERS as it takes
a WHAM from outside.

The Partygoers YELL with every hit.

>   HARPY
>   (to Evelyn)
>   What do they want? Why do they
>   want to hurt us?

>   EVELYN
>   I don't know, Mom. But they do.

Leo commands some MEN.

>   LEO
>   Help me, come on!

The Men lean into the barricade as it takes another BASH.

A SHORT MAN is knocked off balance. Presses again into the
furniture.

>   SHORT MAN
>   How are they so strong?

>   JIMMIE
>   Has to be more than what I saw.
>   Has to be.

Another hit! Part of the barricade collapses.

                         LEO
             Clay! How many you see?

lay crouches to see through.

OV:
reatures, as far as the eye can see.

XT. COMMUNITY CENTER - NIGHT

utside the Community Center, the building is completely
urrounded by an army of Creatures.

t least a hundred. Maybe more.

NT. COMMUNITY CENTER - NIGHT

nother hit!

hairs and tables CRASH DOWN from the pile.

eo and Clay wrench back to avoid being struck.

                    LEO
          Have you got a gun?

                    CLAY
          In my truck.

                    LEO
          Can we get to it?

                    CLAY
          There are probably a dozen guns in
          cars out there, but we're cut off
          from all of them.

eo moves from the barricade, back to Evelyn and her
arents.

                    LEO
                 (re: Jesse)
          Can he stand?

elyn grips her father's arm. Jesse nods.

o and Evelyn raise Jesse up.

rpy hugs her husband tight.

                    HARPY
          We're gonna die, aren't we, Jesse?

                    JESSE
          We'll be okay. You have-- what you
          have here is a room full of life
          experience. Jack there was in the
          Navy -- he might know about sea
          creatures. And Mighty Mick over
          there has 60 years of electrical
          experience. He could make us a
          cattle prod. Hell, that young
          bartender might be able to turn the
          whiskey into Molotov cocktails. If
          only we had Herb Warren and his
          personal armory--

                    LEO
          --Wait-- Yes. How far is Herb's
          place?

                    JESSE
          We'd never make it.

                    LEO
          Maybe a few of us could.

Another hit on the barricade!

                    HARPY
          It's not far if you go over the
          hill. Not the road--

                    JESSE
                 (snaps fingers)
          --Not the road, the woods.

Leo looks to Clay. Read each others' eyes.

                    CLAY
          We don't have much time.

                    LEO
          Then we better go now.

                    EVELYN
          You'll never make it!

The plan is already set in motion.

Leo waves over the Blonde Waiter.

                    LEO
          Come here, kid.

                    BLONDE WAITER
          Yeah.

                    LEO
          You wanna do some good?

                    BLONDE WAITER
          Yeah.

                    LEO
          Clay and I are going to slip out
          the back and run as fast as we can
          for the woods--

                    EVELYN
          --Leo!--

                    LEO
          --and then down the hill to get us
          some firepower. We need you to run
          for the road, try to make it out.
          They may not go after just one
          person. Get to the Visitor's
          Center down the hill. What's that
          guy's name-?

                    CLAY
          --Chuck. Chuck.

                    LEO
          --Tell Chuck to bring the army.

                    BLONDE WAITER
          Yeah.

                    LEO
          You can do that?

     ems REALLY sure.

                    BLONDE WAITER
          Yeah.

                    LEO
          Is that all you ever fucking say?

                    BLONDE WAITER
          What do you want me to say? I'm
          shittin' my pants here.

                         LEO
               Okay, let's stick with 'yeah.'
               Builds confidence.

They break formation, ready to go.

                         HARPY
               This is too dangerous!

The barricade -- BAM!

                         CLAY
               It's gonna be dangerous here if we
               don't get back with some guns.

                         LEO
               Shit. Shit, shit, shit.

He toughs up. Takes a big breath.

                         LEO (CONT'D)
               Ready?

                         CLAY
               Ready.

                         BLONDE WAITER
               Yeah.

EXT. COMMUNITY CENTER - NIGHT

The rear door of the Community Center WHAMS open.

Clay, Leo, and the Blonde Waiter race out into--

--a dense phalanx of Creatures.

Evelyn SCREAMS from the doorway.

                         EVELYN
               No!

Too late!

Creatures are on Clay, Leo, and the Blonde Waiter.

Merciless. Bodies destroyed.

Emboldened, Creatures BURST into the sanctuary of the
Community Center.

Evelyn RETREATS to her parents in the corner.

>   EVELYN (CONT'D)
>   They're here! They're here! Run!

Absolute CHAOS.

Screams, madness.

Partygoers fight with Creatures.

The Community Center is a bloodbath, a montage of horror.

The Female Tender falls backwards through a window, to be devoured by Creatures.

The Short Man makes a break for the broken window, gets outside.

Evelyn spots the escape!

>   EVELYN (CONT'D)
>   The window! The window!

She grabs Harpy and Jesse and PUSHES them towards the hole.

They're beaten to it by Jimmie.

He smashes glass from the window, cuts his hand to make way for them.

Once they're at the window, Jimmie pushes them--

EXT. COMMUNITY CENTER - NIGHT - CONTINUOUS

Outside the Community Center.

Harpy FALLS to the grass. Jesse reaches for her.

>   JESSE
>   Harpy!

Evelyn lifts her mother.

The Creatures have parted, more interested in piling through the decaying barriers.

>   EVELYN
>   Now! We have to go now!

Her parents start for the woods.

She reaches a hand back for Jimmie.

                    JIMMIE
          Go!

                    EVELYN
          Come with us!

                    JIMMIE
          I need to help the others.

                    EVELYN
          These people hate you!

                    JIMMIE
          I need to help them!

He runs back into the battle.

Evelyn can't look.

She takes her father's arm.

And runs.

EXT. WOODS - NIGHT

Evelyn, Jesse, and Harpy stumble through the dark woods,
downhill, cut and scraped by branches and brush.

Behind them, SCREAMS from the Community Center, quieting.

Jesse buckles.

                    EVELYN
          Dad!

                    JESSE
          Let's slow down, honey, okay?

                    HARPY
          You have to keep going. Please.
          Keep going. We're not far enough.

                    JESSE
          What about snakes?

                    EVELYN
          I'll take snakes. Ahh!

Jesse and Evelyn spin to see-!

-Victoria and Shirley Evans, in tears -- dresses ripped and
covered in blood.

velyn grabs them and shoves the two women onward, down the
ill.

                    EVELYN (CONT'D)
          Keep going.

NT. WARREN HOUSE - DUSK

velyn, Harpy, Jesse, and the Evans sisters enter the Warren
ouse -- doors open, lights on.

velyn is the first to see the mutilated body of Linda
arren in her chair.

                    EVELYN
          Don't look, don't look.

he covers her mother's eyes.

                    EVELYN (CONT'D)
          Where did he keep his guns?

                    JESSE
          I-- I think in the basement.

NT. WARREN HOUSE - BASEMENT - NIGHT

erb's basement, the gun collection.

velyn is the first downstairs, and she hurries to the case.

                    EVELYN
          It's unlocked. Thank God.

he takes a pistol from a post. Looks for the bullets.

esse reaches for one, too, but clutches his arm in pain.

rpy guides him to the basement sofa.

                    HARPY
          Sit, sit. You rest. We're gonna
          get help.

                    VICTORIA | SHIRLEY
          Close the door!

Evelyn returns to the top of the stairs.

Gives a last look to the ground floor.

Then, shuts the basement door.

DISSOLVE TO:

INT. WARREN HOUSE - BASEMENT - TIME UNKNOWN

Evelyn, in a recliner, loaded pistol in her hand.

The Evans sisters lay on the floor, each with a Winchester.

Harpy, a Derringer.

Jesse, a double-barrel shotgun set against his leg. White as a sheet, but breathing.

Outside--

--GUNFIRE, distant. Lots of it. Slowing and stopping.

The survivors pass looks.

DISSOLVE TO:

INT. WARREN HOUSE - BASEMENT - TIME UNKNOWN

Evelyn stands.

Pistol in hand, she moves to the stairs.

                    HARPY
                   (soft)
          Evelyn... where you goin;?

                    EVELYN
          It's been quiet for hours.

Up to the top of the basement stairs.

Twists the handle.

Opens the door.

Crouches, pistol ready to fire.

RRRRRRRAAAAAAAAAT!

ullets RIP the wood over Evelyn's head!

velyn DIVES to the ground.

> GUARDSMAN
> Oh, shit!

 battle-ready National GUARDSMAN -- 20s, helmet, uniform,
lack jacket -- stands in the Warren House, hot M-4 Carbine
n his hand.

> GUARDSMAN (CONT'D)
> Shit! I'm sorry, I'm sorry. We
> didn't know you were down there.

wo more GUARDSMEN rush into the room.

> GUARDSMAN (CONT'D)
> Don't shoot, don't shoot! It's a
> person!

he first Guardsman approaches.

> GUARDSMAN (CONT'D)
> Is it just you? Are there others
> down there? What's your name?

velyn rises from the floor.

> HARPY (O.S.)
> Evelyn!

> EVELYN
> I'm okay, Mom!

he dusts herself off.

> GUARDMAN
> Evelyn. Beautiful.

> EVELYN
> (shaking)
> Are those things around?

> GUARDSMAN
> Not here. A lot of 'em have run
> off. We're sweepin' houses.

elyn drops her pistol into a plush chair.

 last, she throws her arms around the Guardsman.

> GUARDSMAN (CONT'D)
> Whoa, whoa, now.

Evelyn cries, can't stop.

He hugs her back.

> GUARDSMAN (CONT'D)
> It's all good. You're all good.

Makes a face to the other Soldiers. What do I do?

At last, Evelyn pulls away.

> GUARDSMAN (CONT'D)
> Hey, hey. Relax. We'll take you
> and your family anywhere you wanna
> go. Where you wanna go?

Evelyn chokes up. Cracks a fond smile.

> EVELYN
> Nashville.

> GUARDSMAN
> That's far. Yeah. Yeah, okay.
> We'll take you to Nashville. I
> always liked Nashville. Country
> music. Pretty girls. Nashville.
> I might go AWOL and stay there with
> you.

Evelyn bends. Breathes. Breathes.

> EVELYN
> Thank you.   Thank you.

When she comes up--

--it's not a Guardsman anymore.

It's a Creature!

Evelyn SCREAMS! Freaks out, nuclear!

She attacks it with her fists, pounds the chest of...

...The Guardsman.

An illusion. PTSD.

                    NATIONAL GUARDSMAN
        Now, now, settle down.   It's over.
        It's over.

he weeps in his arms.

                                BLACKOUT.

                                THE END.

OTHER SCREENPLAYS IN THIS COLLECTION

OTHER SCREENPLAYS IN THIS COLLECTION

ABOUT THE AUTHOR

Darren Callahan is an award-winning writer, director, and composer who has written drama for the BBC, SyFy Channel, National Public Radio, and Radio Pacifica New York. His work for theatre has been both commercially and critically successful and includes several productions in major markets. He began in fiction and became a cult figure for THE AUDREY GREEN CHRONICLES, a series of three interlocking novels, and the epic thriller CITY OF HUMAN REMAINS. His films include UNDER THE TABLE and DESPERATE DOLLS. He has released several dozen records - from pop to noise to ambient to film soundtracks.

His website is darrencallahan.com
WIKIPEDIA is https://en.wikipedia.org/wiki/Darren_Callahan
IMDB is http://www.imdb.me/darrencallahan

Page Intentionally Left Blank

Made in the USA
Monee, IL
15 January 2024

50764476R00072